Keto Diet Cookbook for Beginners After 50

Lose Fat More Easily by Optimizing your Eating Plan,
with Ketogenic Recipes Healthy and Easy to Prepare.
Fight Disease and Slow Aging.
Healthy Living at All Ages.

Mery L. Davis

Table of contents

INTRODUCTION...................5

WHAT IS THE KETOGENIC DIET? 6

WHAT ARE THE BENEFITS OF A KETOGENIC DIET? 6

KETOGENIC FOOD LIST 6

Who is the ketogenic diet suitable for? 9

BREAKFAST 10

Scrambled eggs from the oven.................. 10

Breakfast muffins with egg and bacon 11

Hüttenkase with strawberries.................. 12

Avocado and green tea powershake 13

Paleo breakfast burrito..................... 14

Protein-rich pancakes 15

Mexican scrambled eggs.................... 16

Low-carbohydrate almond waffles........... 17

Cinnamon and coconut pancakes.............. 18

Chia pudding with coconut and strawberries 19

MAIN COURSE 20

Low-carbohydrate bobotie 20

Leek curry casserole with minced meat..... 21

Cauliflower quiche with cheese 22

Low-carbohydrate goulash 23

Low-carbohydrate Shepherd's pie............ 24

Spicy chicken with cauliflower rice........... 26

Low-carbohydrate hot dog sandwich 27

Burrata salad with pesto....................... 28

Greek salad with chicken and tzaziki........ 29

Mexican meatballs 30

Smoked chicken salad.................... 31

Salmon teriyaki with broccoli rice 32

Fish dish with tomato sauce 33

Chicken jambalaya with cauliflower rice ... 34

Chicken siam with cauliflower rice 35

Stuffed zucchini with pizza topping.......... 36

Lettuce wraps with Mexican chicken........ 37

Avocado salad with chicken 38

Indian curry casserole..................... 39

Teriyaki chicken with cauliflower rice 40

Low-carbohydrate enchiladas 41

Stuffed portobello with goat cheese 42

LUNCH 43

Omelette with baby spinach 43

Savory ham cheese muffins 44

Cheese waffles 45

Cream cheese pancakes.......................... 46

Savory egg muffins 47

Low-carbohydrate rösti 48

Forest mushroom soup........................... 49

Low-carbohydrate Chinese chicken salad ..50

Low-carbohydrate flaxseed buns 51

Low-carbohydrate sushi 52

Avocado tuna salad 53

Low-carbohydrate sandwich..................... 54

Courgetti with chicken and pesto.............. 55

Low-carbohydrate detox salad.................. 56

Scrambled eggs with zucchini and shiitake 57

Low-carbohydrate sausage rolls................ 58

Low-carbohydrate caprese salad.............. 59

Lettuce wraps filled with turkey fillet and bacon 60

Low-carb cauliflower couscous 61

Greek salad of grilled halloumi 62

Vitello tonnato 63

Spicy Indian scrambled eggs with spinach . 64

Creamy cauliflower risotto........................ 65

Adam's low-carb bread 66

APPETIZER 67

Low-carbohydrate sajoer beans 67

Fresh cucumber salad 68

Cauliflower salad with cheese................... 69

Fresh green salad...................................... 70

Rutabaga fries 71

Green asparagus with Parma ham 72

Casserole with green beans 73

Sugar snaps from the oven 74

cauliflower Purée 75

Fried Brussels sprouts with pecans............ 76

Low-carb fries... 77

DESSERT AND SNACKS.................................. 78

Low-carb New York cheesecake 78

Low-carbohydrate cake roll with strawberries 79

White chocolate mousse with raspberries.81

Low-carbohydrate eton mess.................... 82

Low-carbohydrate mini tiramisu 83

Low-carbohydrate strawberry flan............ 84

Low-carbohydrate white chocolate cheesecake... 85

Low-carbohydrate coconut pudding.......... 87

Low-carbohydrate chocolate mousse........ 88

Lemon panna cotta 89

Low-carbohydrate almond magnums........ 90

Mascarpone dessert with berries 91

Meringue.. 93

Vanilla coconut ice cream 94

Avocado chocolate cookies 95

Strawberries dipped in chocolate.............. 96

Low-carbohydrate banana muffins 97

Low-carbohydrate apple and cranberry cake 98

Low-carbohydrate cheesecake.................. 99

Vanilla blueberry muffins 100

Chocolate pecan pie 101

CONCLUSION 102

INTRODUCTION

This cookbook is a guide to the ketogenic diet, specially designed for people aged 50 and over.

The ketogenic diet consists of eating foods low in carbohydrates and high in fat, which is used as the main source of energy and burned directly by our body to meet the daily needs, instead of sugars and carbohydrates.

A ketogenic diet is something you should start today for a better lifestyle if you are over 50. Most useful for women, the diet brings benefits for dealing with the symptoms of menopause. Women who are experiencing it, or have experienced it, have a clear idea of the problems that come with it.

The key to success is feeding your body properly instead of filling it with overly processed dishes. In this guide, you'll learn everything you need to know from what to eat when to eat and how to finally feel fit.

After a while, your body will be trained to burn fat, effectively increasing your metabolism.

Instead of focusing on the carbohydrates, you give up, the Keto diet focuses on all the proteins and fats your body craves for. There are many delicious recipes you can follow and foods you can eat, even when you're not at home. The Keto diet is known to be one of the least restrictive diets, which is a key feature to help you follow it so you can lose weight and maintain a healthy body.

This guide will answer all the questions you have about what the menu consists of and how to successfully make Keto a part of your daily life. Unlike other diets, you will be amazed at how much freedom you are still given. It's almost as if you're not on a diet at all!

Over time, your body and brain age, so it's essential to pay attention to how you can successfully maintain your energy levels. Aside from the benefits to your metabolism, you'll also notice decreased inflammation, stable blood sugar levels, and balanced hormones. With all these benefits in place, you'll see that you'll feel better both physically and mentally.

Get ready for an overall lifestyle change that is possible for almost everyone, regardless of your usual day.

Whether you want to maintain your current weight or lose weight, Keto will help you get to where you want to be.

If you are ready to feel good and look great, then you are ready to start your Keto diet. It will be a diet like no other because you will feel great every step of the way. There are no tricks or tricky steps you have to take to be successful with the diet.

Have a great journey!

WHAT IS THE KETOGENIC DIET?

The ketogenic diet is a type of low carb diet and is characterized by the fact that the body learns a new way of generating energy through food.

By consuming a lot of healthy fats and very little carbohydrates, the body enters what is known as "ketosis".

In this state, the body burns fat instead of sugar as fuel for cellular energy. Due to the lack of sugar molecules, the liver is forced to convert fatty acids into so-called " ketone bodies ".

And these ketone bodies are anti-inflammatory and can help you lose weight.

A successfully implemented ketogenic diet must meet the following criteria: The liver produces ketone bodies as an alternative fuel to glucose.

WHAT ARE THE BENEFITS OF A KETOGENIC DIET?

A ketogenic diet always aims to bring the body into so-called " ketosis ". In this ketosis, many people experience several advantages over normal "sugar burning".

But what are the benefits and what is the ketogenic diet used for?

Benefits of the ketogenic diet and ketosis

Anti-inflammatory: The ketogenic diet and the resulting ketosis have a strong anti-inflammatory effect. This is believed to lower the risk of degenerative diseases like Alzheimer's and cancer.

Energy-boosting: The state of ketosis supports the cells, especially the brain, to produce more mitochondria. These mitochondria are the energy power plants of your body and ensure that you are awake and focused from morning to night.

Promotes fat burning: The ketogenic diet can help you lose weight quickly and healthily. The ketone bodies ensure long-term satiety and lowering of hunger hormones (such as ghrelin). This means that you will no longer have food cravings and will no longer have to rely on snacks.

Increases concentration: Ketone bodies are an ideal source of energy for the brain. Once the body has adapted to ketosis, the brain can get up to 75% of the energy from ketone bodies. The brain also benefits from the high consumption of healthy fats, since it consists largely of fat and omega 3 fatty acids that support the health of the brain.

Blood sugar lowering: We receive many testimonials in which people with diabetes report significant improvements in their symptoms. When the ketogenic diet is followed properly, insulin and blood sugar levels stabilize. Important: If you suffer from diabetes, you should have this project accompanied by a doctor who has experience with an LCHF diet before switching.

KETOGENIC FOOD LIST

What foods are keto foods? Our clear ketogenic food list shows you the top 15 ketogenic food groups at a glance:

Meat and poultry

Unprocessed meat contains no carbohydrates, making it perfect for a ketogenic diet. Beef, turkey and chicken provide us with protein and B vitamins. Sausage products such as salami, ham and wieners are also okay if they do not contain any sugary additives or starches.

Note: Reach for products from pasture farming, preferably from organic farms. Avoid too much protein: Prefer high-fat parts, such as pork belly or ribeye.

This is allowed: beef, turkey, chicken, pork, deer, duck, veal, goat, goose, lamb, sheep, turkey, wild boar, offal. Also: salami, ham, Viennese.

Low carb vegetables

Low-carbohydrate vegetables are a major source of vitamins and minerals on the ketogenic food list. Water-rich, green (leaf) vegetables and cabbage vegetables play an important role. With the right choice, you can eat up to 900 g of vegetables a day without affecting ketosis.

Note: Eliminate root vegetables and starchy vegetables such as sweet potatoes, which are high in carbohydrates, from your diet.

This is allowed: Green salads, spinach, broccoli, artichoke, asparagus, cucumber, green peppers, pak choi, Brussels sprouts, white cabbage, cauliflower, Chinese cabbage, kale, celeriac, eggplant, leek, mushrooms, zucchini.

Nuts and seeds

In addition to meat and avocado, natural nuts, seeds and seeds are an important source of fat, which provides us with valuable and essential omega-3 fatty acids and omega-6 fatty acids. They also provide a high-quality nutrient package of minerals such as zinc, iron and magnesium as well as B vitamins. Their filling protein content makes them a great ketogenic snack for in between meals.

Note: Nuts also contain some carbohydrates and will affect your carbohydrate balance. Important: Peanuts are not nutting; they belong to the legume family.

This is allowed: almonds, hazelnuts, macadamia nuts, pecans, walnuts, cashews, pine nuts, pistachios, pumpkin seeds, sesame seeds, sunflower seeds, chia seeds, flax seeds, hemp seeds.

Dark chocolate and cocoa powder

A piece (10 g) of dark chocolate with 85% cocoa provides only 2 g of carbohydrates. Baking or making cocoa with unsweetened cocoa powder will not affect the state of your ketosis.

Note: The high cocoa content in chocolates is mandatory. Use unsweetened cocoa powder that does not contain any other additives.

This is allowed: Chocolate from 70% cocoa, unsweetened cocoa powder, cocoa nibs.

fish

Natural fish is also ketogenic and, in addition to healthy omega-3 fatty acids, provides plenty of protein and keeps you full for a long time. The classic tuna with 0 g of carbohydrates is a very popular, ketogenic food.

Note: Here quality counts instead of quantity: Prefer fresh fish, preferably wild caught and eat it twice a week.

This is allowed: tuna, anchovies, perch, cod, eel, flounder, herring, mackerel, salmon, sardines, turbot, trout, pikeperch, carp, pangasius.

Eggs

Chicken eggs hardly contain any carbohydrates and are rich in protein and vitamins such as A, B and K. Their protein has a high biological value. This provides information about the composition of the amino acids in food and how well these can be used by the body. The higher the value, the better the proteins are metabolized.

Note: For ecological reasons, use organic eggs when buying. For vegetarians, organic eggs are a valuable source of protein in a ketogenic diet. As a meat eater, limit your consumption to prefer proteins from meat and fish.

This is allowed: organic free-range chicken eggs.

cheese

The large selection of different types of cheese also remains with a ketogenic diet. You should primarily choose low-carbohydrate or high-fat cheeses such as camembert, parmesan, feta or mozzarella. But cottage cheese is also established in the ketogenic scene and is a popular and low-fat dip or spread.

Note: Cheese also contains some saturated fat and should only be consumed in moderation. Light products and low-fat cheeses are not ketogenic and therefore taboo.

This is allowed: Harz cheese, sheep cheese, Gouda, mozzarella, Brie, Camembert, Gorgonzola, cottage cheese, ricotta, mascarpone.

Fruit and berries

Finding fruit among the ketogenic foods is not easy. Are allowed berries such as strawberries, and blueberries, carbohydrates 8-10 g per 100 g. And don't forget to include the two rather atypical types of fruit in your diet: avocados and olives.

Note: Tropical fruits contain too much fructose and are not suitable as ketogenic foods.

This is allowed: currants, raspberries, strawberries, cantaloupe, cranberries, blueberries, blackberries, papaya, gooseberries, lemons, limes.

Healthy fats and oils

Medium-chain, so-called MCT fats (Medium Chain Triglycerides) are the keto boosters: They mainly consist of the fatty acids caproic acid, caprylic acid, capric acid and lauric acid and are completely and particularly quickly metabolized. Our body breaks them down directly into ketone bodies. You can use coconut oil here, as it contains many of these fatty acids. Cold-pressed olive oil is great for salads and cold dishes. It not only provides healthy fatty acids, but also has an antioxidant effect.

Note: Prefer pure, cold-pressed and high-quality oils and avoid cheap vegetable products that often contain impurities.

This is allowed: coconut oil, olive oil, MCT oil, avocado oil, macadamia oil, walnut oil, sesame oil, ghee, caprylic acid, cocoa butter, lard, palm oil, nut butter.

Drinks such as unsweetened tea and coffee

Drinking plenty is a must to maintain a healthy water balance and replenish electrolytes. In addition to water, unsweetened teas and coffee are also no problem with a ketogenic diet.

Note: Take a look at the list of ingredients and prefer water and naturally flavored drinks such as cucumber water or tea with fresh ginger.

This is allowed: water, carbonated mineral water, unsweetened tea, herbal teas, unsweetened coffee, cucumber water, coconut milk, nut and almond drinks, bulletproof coffee, lemon and lime juice, vegetable and meat broth.

Dairy products

High fat dairy products are also lower in carbohydrates. They provide you with protein and strengthen your teeth and bones with calcium. So that you can get more sugar from fruits and vegetables, limit your dairy product consumption. Therefore, as with eggs, the following applies: Not too much, unless you are eating a ketogenic vegetarian diet.

Note: Choose fresh, high-quality organic products, even ghee or fresh milk directly from the farm are great, high-quality ketogenic foods.

This is allowed: Whole milk, quark, Greek yogurt, natural yoghurt, cream, sour cream, sour cream.

Seafood and animals

In addition to fresh fish, seafood and animals are also suitable as ketogenic foods. Ketarians particularly value crabs and shrimp for their very low carbohydrate content and high nutrient content. Mussels, for example mussels, are slightly higher in carbohydrates (7 g per 100 g).

Note: Seafood and animals add nutrients to your keto diet, but they are relatively expensive ketogenic foods.

This is allowed: shrimp, caviar, clams, crab, lobster, clams, oysters, shrimp, scallops, squid, lobster, crayfish.

Ketogenic baking ingredients: flours and binders

Traditional flours are not ketogenic, but there are plenty of alternatives that also provide healthy nutrients. However, they behave differently when baking than cereal flours. Many conventional binders such as agar-agar or psyllium husks are also keto-friendly.

Note: Do not directly replace flours in recipes 1: 1 with ketogenic alternatives, as they behave differently.

This is allowed: almond flour, coconut flour, desiccated coconut, psyllium husk flour, pumpkin seed flour, guar flour, carob flour, nut and seed flours, potato fibers, gelatine, apple pectin, psyllium husks, agar gelatin, chia seeds.

Ketogenic sweeteners

Many carbohydrate-free substitute sugars allow coffee or yogurt to be sweetened during a ketogenic diet. The fermented glucose erythritol is tooth-friendly and calorie-free, making it a favorite on the ketogenic food list.

Note: Use artificial sweeteners only in small amounts and treat them as ketogenic "stimulants". Warning: very high consumption can cause gas and diarrhea.

This is allowed: erythritol, stevia, xylitol in small quantities.

Spices and herbs

Spices and herbs add variety to every kitchen - including the ketogenic one. Upgrade the limited food selection with high-quality, pure spices and try out new combinations.

Note: Additives, sugar and flavor enhancers that are not ketogenic can hide in spice mixtures in particular. So, check the list of ingredients carefully.

This is allowed: (Sea) salt, pepper, basil, chili powder, curry, cumin, oregano, thyme, rosemary, sage, turmeric, parsley, coriander, cinnamon, nutmeg, cloves, allspice, ginger, cardamom, paprika, dill.

Who is the ketogenic diet suitable for?

Suitable - medical or nutritional supervision recommended

- athlete
- Overweight
- diabetes
- Pressure to perform
- epileptic
- dementia
- Chronic inflammation
- acne

Unsuitable or only under strict medical or nutritional supervision:

- Biliary problems
- Heart disease
- Thyroid problems
- Underweight
- Increased fat levels in the blood

BREAKFAST

Scrambled eggs from the oven

Cooking time: 25 mins
Total time: 35 mins

INGREDIENTS

- 12 medium eggs
- 300 ml of milk
- 50 gr butter or margarine, melted
- salt and pepper to taste

PREPARATION METHOD

1. Preheat the oven to a hundred seventy-five degree. Pour the melted butter right into a 33 cm x 22 cm baking dish. Now take a large bowl and beat the eggs and salt and pepper. Then add the milk grade by grade simultaneously as you're beating the eggs.
2. When all ingredients are well blended, pour the mixture into the oven dish. Bake the egg mixture inside the preheated oven for 10 minutes. Take the ovenproof dish out of the oven and stir the egg mixture well. Then bake for another 10 to fifteen minutes and serve.

NUTRITIONAL VALUES

Serving Size: 1/6
Calories: 236
Fats: 18.0
Carbohydrates: 3.2
Proteins: 14.2

Breakfast muffins with egg and bacon

Cooking time: 30 mins
Total time: 45 mins

INGREDIENTS

- 4 medium eggs
- 4 slices of bacon or bacon
- 4 tsp melted butter
- 1 slice of cheese
- 2 slices of cheese
- 4 paper aluminum muffin cases
- salt and pepper to taste

PREPARATION METHOD

1. Preheat the oven to a hundred seventy-five degrees. Place the bacon slices in a frying pan and fry over medium heat. Bake until the slice is frivolously browned throughout. Then take away the bacon from the pan and wrap the bacon slices inside the muffin instances.
2. Put a teaspoon of melted butter on the bottom of the muffin tin in each mold. Beat the eggs in a bowl and upload salt and pepper to flavor. Now positioned the eggs in the muffin cups.
3. Place the ramekins on a rack and location within the oven. Bake the bacon and egg truffles within the preheated oven for 10 to 15 minutes. When the muffins are nearly done, vicinity the half slice of cheese on the pinnacle of every muffin and bake them in the oven for some greater minutes till the cheese has melted.

NUTRITIONAL VALUES

Serving Size: 1 muffin
Calories: 174
Fats: 14.3
Carbohydrates: 0.3
Proteins: 10.7

Hüttenkase with strawberries

Cooking time: 10 mins   **Total time: 15 mins**

INGREDIENTS

- 170 gr cottage cheese
- 4 small strawberries
- optional: pinch of cinnamon

- optional: grated sugar-free chocolate
- optional: Sweet Bee honey

PREPARATION METHOD

1. Slice the strawberries on a cutting board. Put the cottage cheese in a bowl and add the strawberries to the bowl. To make the recipe even greater delicious, you can sprinkle a bit of cinnamon and grated sugar-unfastened chocolate over the cottage cheese.

NUTRITIONAL VALUES

Serving Size: 1 bowl
Calories: 14

0Fats: 6.1
Carbohydrates: 6.3

Proteins: 18.0

Avocado and green tea powershake

Cooking time: 5 mins   **Total time: 5 mins**

INGREDIENTS

- 290 ml unsweetened almond milk
- 140 gr Greek yogurt
- 1/2 avocado
- 1/2 scoop vanilla protein powder
- 1 tsp matcha tea powder
- stevia to taste

PREPARATION METHOD

1. Cut the avocado into pieces and positioned the portions inside the blender. Then additionally add the Greek yogurt, protein powder, matcha, and stevia to the blender. Finally, pour the almond milk into the blender. Turn on the blender and blend. Divide the shake between two glasses and enjoy!

NUTRITIONAL VALUES

Serving size: 1 glass   Fat: 16.3   Proteins: 11.3
Calories: 230   Carbohydrates: 6.0

Paleo breakfast burrito

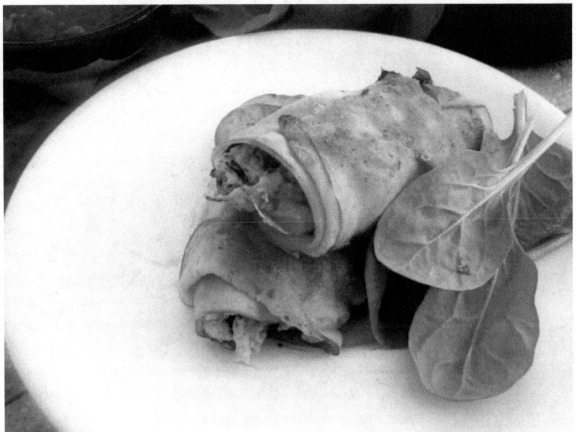

Cooking time: 10 mins   **Total time: 15 mins**

INGREDIENTS

- 6 thick slices of ham
- 4 medium eggs

- 1/2 onion
- 1/2 red bell pepper

- vegetable of your choice
- salt and pepper to taste

PREPARATION METHOD

2. Cut the onion and bell pepper into small portions on a big cutting board. Then fry the onion in a frying pan over medium warmth. After a couple of baking minutes, add the pepper and fry in short.
3. Then pour the eggs over the greens in the pan. Then grasp a spatula and stir properly to make scrambled eggs.
4. Remove the scrambled eggs with the vegetables from the pan. Divide the scrambled eggs and vegetables over the slices of ham and season with salt and pepper. Then roll the ham tightly, and fry the stuffed ham rolls within the frying pan for some seconds.

NUTRITIONAL VALUES

Serving Size: 1 servings   Fat: 12.5   Proteins: 19.8
Calories: 210   Carbohydrates: 4.1

Protein-rich pancakes

Cooking time: 5 mins **Total time: 5 mins**

INGREDIENTS

- 1 bag of Dietimeal pancake mix
- 110 ml of cold water or milk
- 1 tbsp butter
- summer fruits to taste

PREPARATION METHOD

1. Pour the contents of a bag right into a bowl. Add one hundred ten ml of cold water or milk and blend till a homogeneous answer. Heat a tablespoon of butter in a frying pan. Pour the pancake mix into the pan and fry the pancake lightly on each facet for 1 to 3 mins.

NUTRITIONAL VALUES

Serving Size: 1 pancake Fats: 0.2 Proteins: 18.0

Calories: 96 Carbohydrates: 4.1

Mexican scrambled eggs

Cooking time: 10 mins
Total time: 15 mins

INGREDIENTS

- 3 medium eggs
- 30 gr grated cheddar cheese
- 1/2 stalk of spring onion
- 1 - 2 pieces of jalapeños from a jar
- 1/4 onion
- 1/2 Roma tomato
- handful of parsley
- 1 tbsp butter or olive oil
- salt and pepper to taste
- optional: low- carb tortilla

PREPARATION METHOD

1. Cut the spring onions, jalapeños, parsley, and onion into small pieces on a large cutting board. Then take the tomato and cut it into small portions as properly. Place the tomato pieces on a paper towel and drain them in short.
2. Then take a medium bowl and beat the eggs in it. Heat a tablespoon of olive oil in a frying pan and fry the spring onions, onions, and jalapeños. Add the eggs and season with salt and pepper. Let the egg set slowly. As quickly because the egg starts to set at the rims, slide the egg from the threshold to the middle with a spatula and stir the entirety collectively properly.
3. When the scrambled eggs are almost ready, upload the tomato and parsley portions and fry for 1 minute greater. Divide among a plate and garnish with a bit of cheese. Enjoy your meal!

NUTRITIONAL VALUES

Serving Size: 1 portion

Fat: 28.7

Proteins: 21.7

Calories: 365

Carbohydrates: 4.3

Low-carbohydrate almond waffles

Cooking time: 10 mins
Total time: 20 mins

INGREDIENTS

- 2 medium eggs
- 1 small ripe banana
- 100 ml coconut milk
- 75 gr almond flour
- pinch of salt
- 1/2 tsp baking powder
- 1/4 tsp vanilla aroma
- 1/2 tsp cinnamon
- butter or oil for greasing
- optional: 1/2 tbsp psyllium fiber
- optional: Steviala sweetener to taste

PREPARATION METHOD

1. In a large bowl, combine the almond flour, salt, baking powder, vanilla taste, cinnamon, stevia sweetener, and psyllium fiber. Now take any other bowl and mash the banana with a fork. Add the coconut milk and eggs and beat till entire with a whisk.
2. Add the egg mixture to the flour aggregate and beat until smooth. Heat waffle iron and grease it with butter or oil. Add the batter and repeat till you have got made four waffles.

NUTRITIONAL VALUES

Serving Size: 1 wafer
Calories: 208

Fat: 16.9
Carbohydrates: 8.5

Proteins: 7.3

Cinnamon and coconut pancakes

Cooking time: 15 mins   **Total time: 20 mins**

INGREDIENTS

- 2 large eggs
- 1, 5 tablespoons coconut flour
- 1/2 tsp vanilla aroma
- 1/2 tsp cinnamon
- 3/4 tsp baking powder
- 1/2 banana mashed
- 60 ml coconut milk

PREPARATION METHOD

1. In a medium bowl, integrate the eggs, coconut milk, banana, and vanilla flavoring. Then take another bowl and mix inside the cinnamon, coconut flour, and baking powder. Then upload the flour mixture to the egg combination and mix it into a smooth batter.

2. Then take a small frying pan and heat a few butter or oil. Then take a tablespoon of batter and positioned it within the pan. As soon as bubbles shape on the floor of the pancake, turn it over (about a minute and a 1/2 baking). Bake for every other 30 seconds after turning and the pancake is prepared. Repeat this step until you run out of batter.

NUTRITIONAL VALUES

Serving Size: 1 pancake   Fats: 3.8   Proteins: 2.6

Calories: 58   Carbohydrates: 3.3

Chia pudding with coconut and strawberries

Cooking time: 10 mins   **Total time: 20 mins**

INGREDIENTS

- 250 ml unsweetened almond milk or coconut milk
- 3 tbsp chia seeds (25 g)
- 2 tbsp ground coconut
- 1 tsp vanilla aroma
- 1 handful of strawberries, cut into pieces
- Stevia or erythritol to taste

PREPARATION METHOD

1. In a large bowl, mix the almond milk, ground coconut, chia seeds, sweetener, and vanilla aroma properly with a whisk. Divide the mixture over 2 dishes and stand for 10 mins. Stir nicely from time to time throughout the ten minutes. Place the two bowls in the refrigerator in a single day or for at least 2 hours and location the strawberries on the pinnacle of the pudding earlier than serving.

NUTRITIONAL VALUES

Serving Size: 1 bowl   Fat: 18.5   Proteins: 9.4
Calories: 250   Carbohydrates: 3.8

MAIN COURSE
Low-carbohydrate bobotie

Cooking time: 40 mins
Total time: 40 mins

INGREDIENTS

- 250 gr green beans
- 125 gr mushrooms
- 300 gr ground beef, lean
- 1 small onion
- 1 clove of garlic
- 2 eggs
- 100 ml of whole milk
- 2 to 3 tsp curry
- 1 tsp cilantro
- 1/2 tsp ginger
- pinch of cinnamon
- 400 gr of cauliflower rice
- salt and pepper to taste

PREPARATION METHOD

1. Preheat the convection oven to 190 degree. Clean the green beans and remove the ends. Place a pan with water on it and pre-boil the green beans for about 5 mins. Meanwhile reduce the mushrooms, onion and garlic into small pieces.
2. Heat a tablespoon of olive oil in a frying pan and upload the chopped onion, garlic and curry, coriander, ginger, cinnamon, salt and pepper to the pan. Fry this in short and upload the minced meat after 2 mins. Fry the minced meat.
3. Then add the green beans and mushrooms and fry for a couple of minutes. Meanwhile beat the eggs with the milk. Spoon the contents of the pan into a small baking dish and pour the egg mixture over it.
4. Bake the bobotie for approx. 25 to 30 minutes inside the preheated oven. Just before the bobotie is prepared, fry the cauliflower rice in a wok till achieved and season with salt and pepper. Divide the rice and the dish between two plates and enjoy!

NUTRITIONAL VALUES

Serving Size: 1 portion (1/2 of the total)
Calories: 525
Fats: 29.9
Carbohydrates: 13.7
Proteins: 45.2

Leek curry casserole with minced meat

Cooking time: 15 mins
Total time: 35 mins

INGREDIENTS

- 500 gr of lean ground beef
- 125 gr bacon strips
- 4 stalks of leek
- 250 gr mushrooms
- 4 tsp curry powder
- 3 eggs (M)
- 100 ml of whipped cream
- 75 gr grated cheese
- salt and pepper to taste

PREPARATION METHOD

1. Preheat the convection oven to 190 degree.
2. Then add the smoked bacon strips to a frying pan and fry it till crispy. Drain the extra fat after which upload the ground red meat. Fry the minced meat.
3. In the period in-between, cut the mushrooms and leek into small portions and upload this to the frying pan at the side of the curry. Fry the veggies al dente while stirring constantly. Meanwhile beat the eggs in a big bowl with the whipped cream. Add the grated cheese and season with salt and pepper.
4. Put the leek-minced mixture in an oven dish and pour the crushed eggs over it. Bake the oven dish for approx. 25 mins within the preheated oven. Cut the dish into 4 pieces after baking and experience!

NUTRITIONAL VALUES

Serving Size: 1/4 of the dish
Calories: 595
Fats: 42.3
Carbohydrates: 8.7
Proteins: 42.8

Cauliflower quiche with cheese

Cooking time: 50 mins
Total time: 60 mins

INGREDIENTS

- 1 cauliflower
- 1/2 red onion
- 1 red pepper
- 125 gr bacon strips
- 100 gr grated cheese, matured
- 5 eggs (M)
- 125 gr crème fraîche
- paprika to taste
- salt and pepper to taste

1.

PREPARATION METHOD

2. Cut the cauliflower into small florets and add the florets to a pan full of water. Bring this to the boil and prepare dinner for the cauliflower florets for 10 minutes. In the intervening time, fry the bacon until crispy and permit the extra fat to drain after baking.

3. Chop the red onion and the bell pepper and fry it in short in a frying pan with olive oil. Now preheat the convection oven to a hundred ninety degree and grease a quiche pan nicely with butter. Then blend the eggs with the crème fraîche and grated cheese together nicely in a large bowl.

4. Now take the pan with the boiled cauliflower and let the water drain nicely. If necessary, pat the florets dry with a bit of kitchen paper. Add the cauliflower florets alongside the pre-fried bacon, bell pepper, and onion to the bowl with the eggs and stir till nicely blended.

5. Season the batter with salt, paprika, and pepper after which pour it into the greased quiche tin. Bake the cauliflower for approx. 35-40 minutes in the preheated oven until the filling has set. Then cut into 4 pieces and experience!

NUTRITIONAL VALUES

Serving Size: 1/4 of the quiche
Calories: 310
Fat: 24.4
Carbohydrates: 6.2
Proteins: 14.2

Low-carbohydrate goulash

Cooking time: 20 mins
Total time: 1800 mins

INGREDIENTS

- 700 gr of beef steak
- 1 onion
- 2 cloves of garlic
- 30 gr butter
- 1 red pepper
- 1 green pepper
- 400 gr canned tomatoes
- 1 tbsp tomato paste
- 400 gr pumpkin cubes, nutmeg
- 1 beef stock cube
- 200 ml of water
- 1 bay leaf
- 2 tsp paprika powder
- 1 tsp thyme
- 1 tsp caraway seeds
- pinch of black pepper
6.

PREPARATION METHOD

1. Cut the beef and onions into small portions and crush the garlic. Melt the butter in a casserole or skillet and upload the portions of meat. Brown the beef all around after which add the sliced onions and garlic. Bake this for a couple of minutes.
2. Meanwhile, cut the peppers into small pieces and upload this to the pan with the beef. Bake this for a few minutes too. Then upload the tomato paste and herbs to the pan whilst stirring. Deglaze with the water, stock dice, and tomato cubes.
3. Add the bay leaf to the pan and permit the goulash to simmer with the lid on for 2.5 hours over a low warmness. After 2.5 hours of simmering, add the pumpkin cubes and let it simmer for about half-hour, or till the pumpkin is cooked.
4. After simmering, divide the goulash into 4 portions and serve with cauliflower rice if desired. Enjoy your meal!

NUTRITIONAL VALUES

Serving Size: 1 bowl (1/4)

Calories: 401

Fat: 23.5

Carbohydrates: 8.7

Proteins: 34.8

Low-carbohydrate Shepherd's pie

Cooking time: 20 mins
Total time: 40 mins

INGREDIENTS

- Minced meat
- 1 small onion
- 2 cloves of garlic
- 1 carrot
- 1 tbsp olive oil
- 500 gr ground beef
- 1 zucchini
- 400 gr canned tomatoes
- 1 bay leaf
- 1/2 vegetable stock cube
- optional: 2 tsp arrowroot
- salt and pepper to taste

Topping
- 1 small cauliflower
- 20 butter, unsalted
- 50 ml whipped cream
- 50 gr grated cheese for oven gratin
- salt and pepper to taste

PREPARATION METHOD

1. Cut the onion and carrot into small portions and overwhelm the garlic. Heat a tablespoon of olive oil in a massive frying pan and upload the onion and garlic. Saute the onion and garlic until the onions begin to discolor. Then upload the sliced carrot and fry it for a few minutes.
2. Add the floor red meat to the pan and fry it while stirring. Meanwhile reduce the zucchini into small cubes. When the minced meat is cooked, add the zucchini, diced tomatoes, inventory cube, and bay leaf and let it simmer for 10 minutes over low heat, till the sauce has thickened. Then season the minced meat with salt and pepper. You can make the sauce thicker by including a 2 tsp arrowroot.
3. Now preheat the convection oven to one hundred seventy-five degree. Take the cauliflower and cut it into florets. Then bring a pan of water to a boil and add the cauliflower florets. Boil the florets for about 8-10 minutes.
4. Pour the contents of the pan into a colander and allow the florets to drain well. The drier the florets, the better the puree. Then return the drained florets to the pan. Then add the butter, whipped cream, cheese, salt, and pepper to the pan and blend this with a hand blender to an easy puree.
5. Remove the bay leaf from the pan with the minced meat and divide the minced meat over a big oven dish. Spoon the cauliflower puree over this and unfold the puree evenly over the dish with a spoon. Finally, sprinkle the dish with a little cheese
6. Bake the Shepherd pie for 25 minutes in the preheated oven. Cut the pie into 4 identical portions after baking and revel in!
7.

NUTRITIONAL VALUES

Serving size: 1/4 of the total
Calories: 452
Fats: 31.4

Carbohydrates: 10.8
Proteins: 29.4

Spicy chicken with cauliflower rice

Cooking time: 10 mins
Total time: 20 mins

INGREDIENTS

- 300 gr chicken cubes
- 1/2 onion
- 1 clove of garlic
- 3 tbsp sugar-free ketchup
- 2 tbsp soy sauce
- 1 to 2 tsp sambal oelek
- 2 tbsp peanut butter
- optional: 1 tbsp erythritol
- 2 tbsp water
- 400 gr of cauliflower rice
- 1 cucumber
- optional: fried onions

7.

PREPARATION METHOD

1. Cut the onion into small portions on a cutting board and weigh down the garlic. Add a tbsp olive oil to a frying pan and fry the onion and garlic in it. After approximately 2 minutes add the chook cubes and fry them all around.
2. When the chicken cubes are cooked and brown, upload the ketchup, soy sauce, sambal, peanut butter, and erythritol to the pan. Let the contents of the pan simmer for about five minutes, until the sauce has thickened. Add some water if the sauce becomes too thick
3. Meanwhile, fry the cauliflower rice in a separate pan. Cut the cucumber into slices and divide this over two plates together with the rice. Finally, divide the spicy bird over the plates and garnish with spring onions or fried onions. Enjoy your meal!
4.

NUTRITIONAL VALUES

Serving size: 1/2 of the total
Calories: 320
Fat: 8.5

Carbohydrates: 11.8
Proteins: 44.4

Low-carbohydrate hot dog sandwich

Cooking time: 10 mins
Total time: 40 mins

INGREDIENTS

Sandwiches

- 1 egg (M)
- protein from 1 egg (M)
- 100 gr almond flour
- 40 gr melted butter
- 2 tbsp psyllium fiber or 1 tbsp psyllium powder
- 1 tsp baking powder
- 1/2 tsp xanthan gum
- 1/4 tsp salt
- 60 ml of lukewarm water

hotdogs

- 3 fresh hot dogs or frankfurters
- 75 gr mixed raw vegetables with cabbage
- 1 tbsp olive oil
- mustard to taste
- sugar-free ketchup to taste

PREPARATION METHOD

1. Sandwiches. Preheat the convection oven to 175 degrees. Beat the whole egg and the whites together with an electric mixer. While blending, add the last ingredients for the sandwiches to the bowl. Beat the contents of the bowl into an easy or even dough.

2. Divide the dough into 3 balls and shape each ball right into a pistolet form with your fingers. If necessary, wet your fingers to make forming the bun-less complicated. Place the shaped balls on a baking tray coated with parchment paper and bake for 35 mins within the preheated oven.

3. Hotdog. After baking, let the buns calm down and then reduce a small notch inside the middle of the bun. Remove some of the dough inside the bun to make room for the hot canine. Prepare the hot dog or frankfurters in step with the commands on the package.

4. Divide the uncooked greens over the sandwiches and vicinity a warm canine in each sandwich. Garnish the hot canine with sugar-free ketchup, mustard, and every other sauce to taste. Serve and experience!

NUTRITIONAL VALUES

Serving Size: 1 hot dog sandwich
Calories: 547
Fat: 49.8

Carbohydrates: 4.0
Fiber: 6.1
Proteins: 19.7

Burrata salad with pesto

Cooking time: 10 mins
Total time: 20 mins

INGREDIENTS

- 150 gr burrata
- 100 gr arugula salad mix
- 150 gr cherry tomatoes
- 50 gr prosciutto

- 40 gr green pesto
- 1 tbsp olive oil
- handful of pine nuts
- 30 gr Parmesan cheese

8.

PREPARATION METHOD

1. Cut the Parma ham and cherry tomatoes into small pieces on a slicing board. Then, in a small bowl, blend the pesto and olive oil to make the dressing.
2. Divide the salad mixture over plates and beautify with the ham, cherry tomatoes, and parmesan cheese. Then cautiously reduce the burrata in half and vicinity it within the center of each plate.
3. Finally, in short toast the pine nuts in a frying pan and divide this over the plates along with the pesto dressing. Enjoy your meal!

9.

NUTRITIONAL VALUES

Serving size: 1/2 of the total
Calories: 490
Fats: 40.9

Carbohydrates: 7.1
Proteins: 21.8

Greek salad with chicken and tzaziki

Cooking time: 70 mins
Total time: 70 mins

INGREDIENTS

- Salad
- 300 gr chicken tenderloins
- 1/2 red onion
- 1 cucumber
- 3 tomatoes
- 12 olives
- 60 gr feta
- 100 gr tzatziki

- Chicken marinade
- 3 tbsp sour cream
- 1 clove of garlic, crushed
- 2 tbsp olive oil
- 1 tbsp lemon juice
- 2 tsp oregano
- 3/4 tsp salt
- 1/2 tsp black pepper

PREPARATION METHOD

1. In a huge bowl, combine the substances for the chicken marinade. Add the hen breast strips to the bowl and cover with hold film. Put the bowl in the refrigerator and permit the marinade to soak for a minimum of an hour.
2. Heat a tablespoon of olive oil in a frying pan or grease a grill with a bit of oil. Place the strips with a spatula inside the frying pan or grill and bake them for about 6-eight minutes.
3. Meanwhile, reduce the cucumber and tomato into cubes. Then take the red onion and cut it into cubes or earrings. Divide the vegetables among bowls and add the feta, olives, and tzatziki.
4. Let the chicken strips calm down after baking and then upload them to the bowl. Garnish the salad with a bit of sparkling parsley if desired. Enjoy your meal!

Mexican meatballs

Cooking time: 10 mins
Total time: 20 mins

INGREDIENTS

- Meatballs
- 500 gr ground beef
- 1 tbsp almond flour
- 1 jalapeño pepper
- 85 grams of grated cheddar
- 1 egg (M)
- 1 clove of garlic pressed
- 2 tsp cumin
- 2 tsp chili powder
- 1 tsp paprika powder
- 1/2 tsp salt
- Salsa
- 1 can of peeled tomatoes (400 gr)
- 1 jalapeño pepper, finely chopped
- 1/2 onion, finely chopped
- 1 clove of garlic, crushed

- lime juice to taste
- 1 tsp cumin
- 1 tsp salt
- handful of parsley, finely chopped

PREPARATION METHOD

1. Meatballs. Preheat the convection oven to one hundred ninety ranges. Cut the jalapeño pepper into small pieces on a large reducing board. Add the chopped pepper to a large bowl in conjunction with the remaining meatball elements.
2. Mix the substances nicely with your arms inside the bowl. Shape the minced meat into approx. 15 meatballs. Place the balls on a baking tray protected with parchment paper. Bake the balls for about 20 mins in the preheated oven.
3. Salsa. Meanwhile, make the salsa by way of including all of the salsa ingredients in a blender. Turn at the blender till the salsa has the preferred consistency. Add the salsa to a bowl and placed it blanketed within the refrigerator for some time.
4. Serve the meatballs with salsa and sour cream and spring onion if favored. Enjoy your meal!

NUTRITIONAL VALUES

Serving Size: 1 meatball with salsa
Calories: 95
Fat: 5.8

Carbohydrates: 1.5
Proteins: 8.9

Smoked chicken salad

Cooking time: 15 mins
Total time: 20 mins

INGREDIENTS

- Salad
- 100 gr salad mix
- 150 gr smoked chicken fillet slices
- 2 vine tomatoes
- 100 gr bacon strips
- 150 gr mini mozzarella balls

- 1/2 cucumber
- Yogurt mayonnaise dressing
- 4 tbsp whole yogurt
- 2 tbsp mayonnaise
- 1 tsp mustard

PREPARATION METHOD

1. Cut the tomatoes and cucumber into small cubes on a large slicing board. Then warmness a frying pan over medium warmth and upload the bacon. Fry the bacon for approximately 5 mins until golden brown and crispy.
2. Add the salad blend, smoked chicken, and mini mozzarella balls to a massive bowl. Mix the entirety together nicely and upload the chopped vegetables and the cooled bacon cubes.
3. Now make the dressing by using mixing the yogurt, mayonnaise, and mustard nicely in a bowl. Divide the salad between plates and serve with a yogurt mayonnaise dressing. Enjoy your meal!

NUTRITIONAL VALUES

Serving Size: 1 portion (1/2 of the total)
Calories: 506
Fat: 36.0

Carbohydrates: 5.4
Proteins: 39.5

Salmon teriyaki with broccoli rice

Cooking time: 15 mins
Total time: 25 mins

INGREDIENTS

Salmon teriyaki

- 2 salmon fillets
- 50 ml soy sauce
- 50 ml of water
- 1 clove of garlic, finely crushed
- 3 cm fresh ginger, grated
- 1 tbsp wok oil
- 1 tsp arrowroot
- optional: 1 tbsp erythritol
- 1 tbsp sesame seeds
10. Broccoli rice
- 400 gr broccoli rice
- 1 tbsp olive oil
- 1 shallot
- 2 lemon slices
- 1 stalk of spring onion
- salt and pepper to taste

PREPARATION METHOD

1. Preheat the oven to 180 degree. In a small saucepan, combine the soy sauce, beaten garlic, grated ginger, wok oil, arrowroot, and water. Put the pan at the range and convey it to a boil. Let it boil for approximately 2-three minutes until the sauce has thickened slightly.
2. Place the salmon fillets in a small oven dish and pour the sauce over the salmon fillets. Now take a spoon or kitchen brush and coat the zam fillets properly with the sauce in the dish. Bake the salmon teriyaki within the preheated oven for 15 minutes.
3. Meanwhile, finely chop a shallot and fry it in a frying pan with olive oil. Add the broccoli rice and wok it inside four-5 mins. Season the rice with salt and pepper. Divide the broccoli rice between plates and set aside.
4. After baking, location the salmon fillets on the broccoli rice and garnish with chopped spring onions and sesame seeds. Serve the salmon fillets with a slice of lemon if favored. Enjoy your meal!

NUTRITIONAL VALUES

Serving size: 1/2 of the total

Calories: 530

Proteins: 38.4

Fats: 37.8

Carbohydrates: 5.4

Fish dish with tomato sauce

Cooking time: 30 mins
Total time: 45 mins

INGREDIENTS

- 1 cauliflower
- 1 vegetable stock cube
- 2 tins of peeled tomatoes (800 gr)
- 2 cloves of garlic, finely crushed
- 4 tbsp olive oil
- 500 grams of cod
- 250 gr mozzarela (bulb)
- 1/2 lemon
- 1 sprig of parsley
- salt and pepper to taste

PREPARATION METHOD

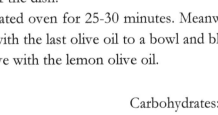

1. Preheat the oven to two hundred degree. Add the peeled canned tomatoes to a big stockpot and mash it finely with a hand blender. Season the tomato sauce with salt and pepper and upload 2 tbsp olive oil and the beaten garlic. Bring the sauce to the boil and cook for about five-10 mins, until the sauce has thickened properly.
2. Meanwhile, reduce the cauliflower into florets and upload the florets to a pan full of water. Add the inventory dice and bring the water to a boil. Cook the cauliflower for approx. 10 minutes until al dente and then permit the water drain.
3. Add the tomato sauce to a big casserole dish and place the cod within the sauce. Season the cod and sauce with salt and pepper. Then additionally upload the cauliflower florets. Tear the mozzarella into small portions and spread calmly over the dish.
4. Bake the fish dish in the preheated oven for 25-30 minutes. Meanwhile, grate the lemon and finely chop the parsley. Add this together with the last olive oil to a bowl and blend properly. After baking, divide the dish into four portions and serve with the lemon olive oil.

NUTRITIONAL VALUES

Serving Size: 1/4 of the dish
Calories: 400
Fats: 23.6

Carbohydrates: 9.3
Proteins: 35.3

Chicken jambalaya with cauliflower rice

Cooking time: 15 mins
Total time: 30 mins

INGREDIENTS

- 300 gr chicken fillet
- 125 gr chorizo
- 1 onion
- 1 clove of garlic
- 1/2 red bell pepper
- 1 tbsp tomato paste
- 2 large tomatoes
- 1 tsp paprika powder
- 1 tsp cajun seasoning
- salt and pepper to taste
- parsley to taste
- 600 gr cauliflower rice

PREPARATION METHOD

1. Cut the onion into small pieces and weigh down the garlic. Then cut the bird breast and chorizo into small cubes and set them aside. Heat a tbsp olive oil in a large wok pan and fry the onion and garlic in it until the onion starts off evolved to discolor. Then add the chicken and herbs and fry the chicken till done.
2. In the intervening time, cut the bell pepper and tomato into small cubes and add this to the chicken together with the chorizo. Fry this in short and then add a tablespoon of tomato puree to the pan. Fry the contents of the pan inside approx. Five mins even as stirring.
3. Meanwhile, fry the cauliflower rice in every other pan. Add this to the pan with the hen and chorizo and fry it in short. Divide the bird jambalaya between 3 plates and season with salt, pepper, and sparkling parsley. Enjoy your meal!

NUTRITIONAL VALUES

Serving Size: 1 portion (1/3)
Calories: 347
Fat: 16.6Carbohydrates: 9.8
Fiber: 5.1
Proteins: 36.8

Chicken siam with cauliflower rice

Cooking time: 15 mins
Total time: 25 mins

INGREDIENTS

- 500 gr chicken fillet cubes
- 400 gr of cauliflower rice
- 1 red pepper
- 2 cloves of garlic
- 1 cm ginger
- 1/2 onion
- 3 tbsp olive oil
- 3 tbsp oyster sauce
- 1 tbsp soy sauce
- 50 ml of water
- 2 tsp arrowroot
- 2 stalks of spring onion
- 40 gr cashew nuts

PREPARATION METHOD

1. Finely chop the ginger and onion on a slicing board. Then warmness the olive oil in a massive frying pan. Add the chook cubes and stir-fry for about 3-6 minutes till accomplished. Then crush the garlic and upload it to the pan along with the onion and ginger. Fry the seasonings for three minutes.
2. In the interim, reduce the bell pepper into small pieces after which upload this to the pan. In a small bowl, mix the water, oyster sauce, and soy sauce together and add this to the chicken and vegetables.
3. Then mix in a tumbler a tbsp water with 2 tsp arrowroot and upload this to the pan to thicken the sauce. Boil the contents of the pan for 2-3 mins, until the sauce has thickened. Finally, stir the cashews into the pan.
4. Now warmth a tbsp olive oil in a new pan and wok the cauliflower rice till accomplished. Finely chop the spring onion and set it apart. Divide the cauliflower rice over four plates and spoon the hen siam over it. Garnish with the sliced spring onion. Enjoy your meal!

NUTRITIONAL VALUES

Serving size: 1/4 of the total
Calories: 308
Fats: 13.7
Carbohydrates: 9.8
Proteins: 34.2

Stuffed zucchini with pizza topping

Cooking time: 15 mins
Total time: 25 mins

INGREDIENTS

- 2 courgettes
- 200 gr tomato sauce
- 1/4 red onion
- 1/2 green pepper
- 125 gr mushrooms
- 60 gr salami
- 80 gr grated mozzarella
- Italian herbs to taste
- salt and pepper to taste

PREPARATION METHOD

1. Preheat the convection oven to two hundred degrees. Wash the courgettes and cut them in half lengthwise. Remove the flesh with a spoon and set it aside. Then cut the green pepper, mushrooms, onion, and salami into small pieces.
2. Take the zucchini and place it in a greased oven dish. Fill the 4 hollowed-out courgettes with the tomato sauce. Then divide the sliced veggies and salami over the courgettes. Season the crammed zucchini with Italian herbs, salt, and pepper.
3. Finally, sprinkle the courgettes with grated mozzarella and cowl the dish with aluminum foil. Bake the courgettes in the preheated oven for 15 mins. Then remove the foil and bake for every other 10 minutes.

NUTRITIONAL VALUES

Serving Size: 2 pieces of stuffed zucchini
Calories: 338
Fats: 19.6
Carbohydrates: 15.8
Proteins: 22.3

Lettuce wraps with Mexican chicken

Cooking time: 10 mins
Total time: 70 mins

INGREDIENTS

Chicken marinade

- 300 gr chicken fillet
- 2 tbsp olive oil
- 1 tbsp lime juice
- 1 tbsp Taco seasoning
- 1/2 tsp ground coriander
- 1/2 tsp dried oregano
- salt and pepper to taste
- wraps
- 1 head of romaine lettuce
- 1 avocado
- 1/2 red onion
- 1/2 cucumber
- 250 gr cherry tomatoes

Sauce

- 125 ml of sour cream
- 1 tbsp mayonnaise
- handful of fresh parsley
- 1/2 tbsp lime juice
- 1/4 tsp cumin powder
- 1/4 tsp garlic powder

PREPARATION METHOD

1. In a huge bowl, mix the herbs properly collectively for the marinade. Add the olive oil and blend properly once more. Cut the chicken into cubes if essential and add this to the marinade. Put the bowl inside the fridge and allow the marinade to soak for at least an hour.
2. Meanwhile, in a bowl, mix all the substances for the sauce collectively with a whisk. Cover the bowl with cling movie and placed it in the fridge. Then reduce the avocado, cucumber, cherry tomatoes, and onion into small portions.
3. Then take the bowl with the chicken from the refrigerator. Heat a tablespoon of olive oil in a frying pan and add the bird and marinade to the pan. Fry the hen in approximately 10 mins until brown and done.
4. Place some of the lettuce leaves in a row on a huge shelf and fill them with the sliced greens and chicken. Garnish with the sauce and serve. Enjoy your meal!

NUTRITIONAL VALUES

Serving Size: 2 lettuce wraps
Calories: 359
Fats: 22.8

Carbohydrates: 7.4
Proteins: 28.4

Avocado salad with chicken

Cooking time: 30 mins
Total time: 30 mins

INGREDIENTS

Chicken

- 300 gr chicken fillet (cubes)
- 1 tbsp olive oil
- 1/2 tsp salt and black pepper
- 1/4 tsp paprika powder
- 1/8 tsp onion powder
- 1/4 tsp garlic powder
- 1/8 tsp cumin powder
- 1/4 tsp chili powder
- 1/8 tsp oregano
- lemon juice from 1/2 lemon

Salad

- 1 cucumber
- 1 avocado
- 250 gr cherry tomatoes
- 1/4 red onion
- 3 tbsp lime juice
- 2 tbsp olive oil
- salt and pepper to taste

PREPARATION METHOD

1. In a large bowl, blend all the herbs for the marinade collectively with olive oil and lemon juice. Add the chook fillet (cubes) to the bowl and put it inside the refrigerator. Let the marinade sit down for at least 15 mins.
2. Fry the marinated hen in a frying pan, grill pan, or at the barbecue. In the intervening time, reduce the cucumber, avocado, and cherry tomatoes into pieces. Chop the onion and upload the vegetables to a bowl.
3. After baking, reduce the chicken fillet into cubes and upload it to the bowl with the vegetables. Mix the contents of the bowl nicely. Then make the dressing by mixing the lime juice and olive oil in a small bowl.
4. Divide the salad among two plates and serve with the fresh lime dressing. Enjoy your meal!

NUTRITIONAL VALUES

Serving size: 1/2 of the total
Calories: 438
Fat: 13.0

Carbohydrates: 8.4
Fiber: 5.7
Proteins: 39.1

Indian curry casserole

Cooking time: 40 mins
Total time: 60 mins

INGREDIENTS

Casserole

- 600 gr chicken thigh fillet
- 1 cauliflower
- 2 tbsp olive oil
- 1 tin of diced tomatoes (400 gr)
- 200 ml coconut milk
- 1 tbsp tomato paste
- 1/2 cube of chicken stock
- salt and pepper to taste
- 100 g baby spinach
- 200 gr green beans

Curry paste

- 2 tbsp grated ginger
- 1/2 onion
- 2 cloves of garlic
- 1 tsp ground cumin
- 1 tsp turmeric
- coriander to taste
- 1/2 tsp paprika
- 1/2 tsp garam masala
- 1 red pepper, finely chopped

PREPARATION METHOD

1. Preheat the convection oven to one hundred eighty degrees. Cut the cauliflower into florets. Bring a pan of water to the boil and cook the cauliflower for 5 mins until soft. After cooking, let it drain properly and location it in a greased oven dish together with the bird thigh fillet. Drizzle the cauliflower and chook with olive oil and season with salt and pepper. Bake the dish for approx. 25 minutes in the preheated oven.

2. Meanwhile, make the curry paste by mixing all of the elements in a blender. Add the curry paste to a skillet and cook dinner for 1 minute. Then upload a tbsp olive oil and fry for every other minute. Then take the tomato paste, diced tomatoes, coconut milk, and the chicken stock and add this to the curry paste. Let this simmer for 5 mins over low heat whilst stirring. Taste the sauce and add more salt or pepper if important.

3. Stir fry the spinach in a frying pan for two-three minutes and upload it to the sauce. Remove the casserole with the fried chicken from the oven and take a look at if the chicken is cooked. Add the curry sauce and bake the dish for another 10 minutes within the preheated oven.

4. Meanwhile, carry a pan of water to a boil and add the green beans. Cook the green beans for 5-10 mins al dente. Serve the curry dish with the cooked green beans and a bit of Greek yogurt if favored. Enjoy your meal!

NUTRITIONAL VALUES

Serving Size: 1/4 of the dish
Calories: 402
Fats: 23.9

Carbohydrates: 9.3
Fiber: 6.4
Proteins: 34.4

Teriyaki chicken with cauliflower rice

Cooking time: 20 mins
Total time: 40 mins

INGREDIENTS

Marinade

- 1 tbsp wok oil
- 1 clove of garlic,
- 3 cm fresh ginger
- 1 tbsp sesame seeds
- 30 ml soy sauce
- 30 ml of water
- 1 tbsp erythritol
- optional 1/4 tsp xanthan gum

Teriyaki

- 300 gr chicken fillet cubes
- 400 gr broccoli florets
- 1 tbsp wok oil
- 1/2 onion
- 250 gr sliced mushrooms

- 400 gr of cauliflower rice
- 1 stalk of spring onion
- 2 tbsp sesame seeds
- optional: 1 red pepper

PREPARATION METHOD

1. Using a garlic press, press the clove of garlic into a pulp. Then take a small grater and grate the ginger with it. Heat a tablespoon of wok oil in a massive frying pan and upload the garlic, ginger, and sesame seeds. Fry this for 1 minute over an excessive warmness and then upload the soy sauce, water, and erythritol. Reduce warmth and simmer for 2 mins. Finally, upload the xanthan gum and heat it until the sauce has thickened.

2. Let the marinade settle down and then upload it to a bowl in conjunction with all of the chicken cubes. Cover the bowl and let the marinade relax in the fridge for at least 15 mins.

3. Meanwhile, finely chop the onion and heat a tablespoon of wok oil in a big frying pan. Add the onion to the pan and fry it till it starts to discolor. Spoon the hen with the marinade into the pan and fry all of it round until carried out and golden brown.

4. Add the sliced mushrooms and fry for 2-three mins. Add a finely chopped pink pepper for greater highly spiced teriyaki. In the period in-between, carry a pan of water to the boil and add the broccoli florets. Boil the florets with a lid on the pan for 3-4 minutes till gentle.

5. Then take every other frying pan and wok the cauliflower rice until accomplished. Divide the chicken teriyaki, cauliflower rice, and cooked broccoli among plates and garnish with chopped spring onion and sesame seeds. Enjoy your meal!

NUTRITIONAL VALUES

Serving size: 1/2 of the total

Calories: 431

Fats: 16.2

Carbohydrates: 9.4

Fiber: 12.2

Proteins: 51.5

Low-carbohydrate enchiladas

Cooking time: 25 mins
Total time: 50 mins

INGREDIENTS

Cauliflower tortillas

- 400 gr of cauliflower rice
- 3 eggs (M)
- 1/2 tsp salt
- 1/4 tsp black pepper

Enchilada sauce

- 3 tbsp olive oil
- 2 tbsp arrowroot powder
- 1 can of tomato pulp or cubes
- 350 ml of water
- 1/2 vegetable stock cube
- 1/2 tsp chili powder
- 1/4 tsp ground cumin
- 1/4 tsp garlic powder
- salt and pepper to taste

Stuffing

- 500 gr chicken fillet
- 150 gr mozzarella

PREPARATION METHOD

1. For approximately 20 minutes. Remove the bird breasts from the pan and pull them aside with spoons to make pulled chook.
2. Preheat the convection oven to a hundred and eighty degree. Heat a tablespoon of olive oil in a large frying pan and upload the cauliflower rice. Wok the rice for about 3 minutes. Add the rice to an easy tea towel or cheesecloth and let it quiet down. Then squeeze the moisture out of the rice and add the rice to a bowl.
3. Add the eggs, salt, and pepper to the bowl and mix nicely. Cover a baking tray with parchment paper and scoop eight piles onto the baking tray. Form 8 tortillas from the mounds and bake for 10 minutes inside the preheated oven. Then flip the tortillas and bake for every other 5 minutes. If all the tortillas do not suit the plate, you can bake it in. Then fry the tortillas in the frying pan for two minutes for a brown crust.
4. Heat three tbsp olive oil in a pan and upload the arrowroot and chili powder. Fry this for two mins even as stirring after which upload the tomato pulp, water, and other herbs. Reduce warmth and simmer for 10 minutes.
5. Take the casserole and grease it with oil. Add a few tablespoons of sauce and region tortillas on top. Then upload the pulled bird, cheese, and a touch sauce. Repeat this till all components are used.
6. Cover the dish with aluminum foil and bake for 30 minutes in the preheated oven. Remove the foil from the dish and bake for any other five mins. Divide the enchiladas among four plates and serve with spring onion, crème fraîche, and guacamole if desired.

NUTRITIONAL VALUES

Serving Size: 1/4 of the dish

Fat: 45.9

Proteins: 45.9

Calories: 420

Carbohydrates: 10.1

Stuffed portobello with goat cheese

Cooking time: 30 mins
Total time: 40 mins

INGREDIENTS

- 4 portobellos
- 2 shallots
- 2 cloves of garlic
- dash of olive oil
- 100 g baby spinach
- 200 gr tomato pulp or cubes
- 1 tbsp Italian herbs
- 100 gr goat cheese
- handful of chopped walnuts
- salt and pepper to taste
- optional: spring onion

PREPARATION METHOD

1. Heat the convection oven to two hundred degree. Cover a baking tray with parchment paper and lightly grease it with a touch of olive oil. Clean the portobello mushrooms with a paper towel and carefully cast off the stem. Then vicinity the mushrooms with the stem dealing with up at the baking tray. Spread the mushrooms with olive oil and season with salt and pepper to taste. Bake the portobello mushrooms inside the preheated oven for 10-15 minutes.

2. In the period in-between, reduce the shallots into small pieces and weigh down the garlic with a garlic press. Heat a tablespoon of olive oil in a big frying pan and add half of the sliced shallot and crushed garlic. Fry for a minute, till the onion starts to discolor. Then add the spinach and fry for 2-three minutes. Season with salt and pepper and set aside.

3. Now take a brand-new pan and fry the relaxation of the chopped shallot and crushed garlic in it. Add the tomato pulp or diced tomatoes and cook for 5-10 minutes, till the sauce has decreased and thickened. Season the sauce with salt, pepper, and Italian herbs.

4. Remove the portobello mushrooms from the oven and pat them dry with a paper towel. Then divide the tomato sauce evenly over the mushrooms. Add the spinach and eventually the chunks of goat cheese. Bake the portobello mushrooms within the preheated oven for every other 15 mins.

5. After baking for 10 mins, upload chopped walnuts and cook dinner for any other five mins. After baking, garnish the stuffed portobello mushrooms with finely chopped spring onion. Enjoy your meal!

NUTRITIONAL VALUES

Serving Size: 2 stuffed portobello mushrooms

Calories: 345

Fats: 24.1

Carbohydrates: 13.4

Proteins: 16.2

LUNCH

Omelette with baby spinach

Cooking time: 10 mins
Total time: 25 mins

INGREDIENTS

- 2 - 3 medium eggs
- 30 g baby spinach, cut into pieces
- 10 gr Parmesan cheese, grated

- 1/4 tsp onion powder
- 1/8 tsp nutmeg
- salt and pepper to taste

PREPARATION METHOD

1. In a massive bowl, beat the eggs and add the spinach and Parmesan cheese whilst stirring. Season with onion powder, nutmeg, salt, and pepper.
2. Grease a small skillet with butter or oil and warm the pan over medium warmth. Add the egg aggregate to the pan and cook dinner the omelet on one aspect for approximately 3 minutes. Then turn the omelet with a spatula and fry for every other three minutes. Now decrease the heat and cook for any other 2 minutes. Enjoy your meal!

NUTRITIONAL VALUES

Serving Size: 1 omelet
Calories: 186
Fats: 12.7

Carbohydrates: 2.9
Proteins: 17.0

Savory ham cheese muffins

Cooking time: 10 mins
Total time: 35 mins

INGREDIENTS

- 125 gr ham cubes
- 125 gr grated cheese
- 4 medium eggs
- 45 gr green pepper
- 1 celery stalk
- 1 tbsp chives, finely chopped
- 1 tbsp parsley, finely chopped
- 1/4 tsp onion powder
- 1/4 tsp pepper

PREPARATION METHOD

1. Preheat the oven to one hundred eighty degrees. Cut the bell pepper and celery into small pieces on a huge slicing board. Then grind the ham in a food processor. Then mix all components in a huge bowl.
2. Divide the mixture from the bowl over the 6 muffin cups. Place the aluminum muffin cases on an oven rack lined with parchment paper. Bake the cakes inside the preheated oven for approximately 25-half-hour until golden brown. Let the truffles cool at the rack for 10 mins. Remove the muffins from the tin and serve.

NUTRITIONAL VALUES

Serving Size: 1 muffin
Calories: 157
Fat: 11.3
Carbohydrates: 1.8
Proteins: 11.7

Cheese waffles

Cooking time: 18 mins
Total time: 28 mins

INGREDIENTS

- 100 g cauliflower, finely ground
- 110 gr grated mozzarella cheese, finely ground
- 35 gr grated Parmesan cheese
- 2 medium eggs
- 1 tbsp chives
- 1 tsp garlic powder
- 1 tsp onion powder
- 1/2 tsp black pepper

PREPARATION METHOD

1. In a large bowl, mix all elements well. Then warmth the waffle iron. Place 1/4 cup of the batter inside the waffle iron. Bake the waffles for 4 to 6 mins.
2. If the waffles still keep on with the iron after 6 mins, let them bake for a while. Repeat this till you have baked four waffles. Let the waffles cool on a plate and positioned the waffles you may not consume inside the fridge.

NUTRITIONAL VALUES

Serving Size: 1 wafer
Calories: 160
Fats: 11.2
Carbohydrates: 1.7
Proteins: 13.2

Cream cheese pancakes

Cooking time: 10 mins
Total time: 15 mins

INGREDIENTS

- 55 gr cream cheese
- 2 medium eggs
- 1/2 tsp cinnamon
- stevia or erythritol to taste

PREPARATION METHOD

1. Place all elements in a blender or food processor. Turn on the blender and mix until clean. After blending, permit the batter to rest outdoor in the fridge for 2 mins.
2. Heat a greased skillet over medium heat. You can select to bake one big pancake or two to 3 small ones. Add the butter and fry the pancake till bubbles seem on the top of the pancake and the rims are dry. Then turn the pancake and bake it for every other 1 minute

NUTRITIONAL VALUES

Serving Size: 1 large pancake
Calories: 344
Fats: 29.1
Carbohydrates: 2.5
Proteins: 17.2

Savory egg muffins

Cooking time: 35 mins   **Total time: 45 mins**

INGREDIENTS

- 6 medium eggs
- 100 gr of lean ground beef
- 1 small onion
- 1/2 red bell pepper

- handful of fresh spinach
- 1 clove of garlic, finely crushed
- 1 tbsp coconut oil
- 2 tsp tomato paste

- 1/2 tsp finely ground cumin
- salt and pepper to taste

PREPARATION METHOD

1. Preheat the oven to 180 ° C and grease a muffin tin with 6 ramekins with a bit of coconut oil. Then beat the eggs in a bowl and mix in the tomato puree, salt, and pepper.

2. Melt a tablespoon of coconut oil in a massive frying pan over medium warmness and sauté the onion in it. Add the finely beaten garlic, minced meat, and cumin and fry for 5-10 mins on low warmth. Finally, add the bell pepper and spinach and fry it briefly.

3. Remove the frying pan from the warmth and upload the minced meat aggregate to the egg combination and stir nicely. Then pour the egg aggregate into the muffin tin and bake the egg desserts for 15-25 mins in the preheated oven or until a skewer comes out clean. Enjoy your meal!

NUTRITIONAL VALUES

Serving Size: 1 muffin   Fat: 8.2   Proteins: 9.4

Calories: 153   Carbohydrates: 4.0

Low-carbohydrate rösti

Cooking time: 10 mins
Total time: 25 mins

INGREDIENTS

- 150 gr celeriac
- 1 tbsp olive oil
- 1 tbsp butter
- 15 g bacon, cut into small pieces
- 20 gr grated Parmesan cheese
- 1/2 tsp salt
- 1/8 tsp ground black pepper
- 1/4 tsp garlic powder
- handful of lamb's lettuce

PREPARATION METHOD

1. To start with, snatch the celeriac. Place the celeriac on a large slicing board and reduce the tuber in half. Then placed the celeriac flat jug on the board and thoroughly cut the skin away, till you're left with only the white flesh.
2. Then take a massive grater and grate a piece of the celeriac over a bowl. Grate the celeriac until you've got one hundred fifty grams of grated pulp. Add the parmesan cheese and the herbs and blend nicely.
3. Then heat the olive oil and butter in a frying pan over medium heat. Add the bacon and fry it crispy. Then add the celeriac mixture to the pan and press with the return of a big spoon at the aggregate to form a massive pancake.
4. Fry the rösti over medium to low warmth for approximately five mins. Until the bottom is golden brown and crispy. When the rösti is ready, take away the pain from the warmth and keep it the wrong way up over a plate, and punctiliously permit the rösti to fall. Serve the low-carb rösti warm or cold with a few lamb's lettuces!

NUTRITIONAL VALUES

Serving Size: 1 rösti
Calories: 332
Fats: 21.0

Carbohydrates: 8.3
Proteins: 13.3

Forest mushroom soup

Cooking time: 30 mins
Total time: 45 mins

INGREDIENTS

- 200 gr mushroom mix, sliced
- 125 ml of whipped cream
- 1 - 2 shallots
- 2 vegetable stock cubes
- 1 handful of fresh parsley
- optional: a drop of olive oil with truffle flavor

PREPARATION METHOD

1. Finely chop the shallots and fry them in a massive frying pan with olive oil. When the shallots flip color, add the mushroom mixture and fry briefly. Then take a huge stockpot and produce 1 liter of water to the boil.
2. When the water is boiling, upload the stock cubes to the stockpot and stir nicely. Add 3/4 of the baked mushroom mix, all of the shallots, and a hundred twenty-five ml of whipped cream to the stockpot and allow it to simmer for approximately 10 minutes on low heat.
3. After cooking for 10 minutes, puree the soup with a hand blender or blender. After blending, stir the last 1/four of the fried mushroom mixture into the soup and add chopped clean parsley. Enjoy your meal!

NUTRITIONAL VALUES

Serving Size: 1 bowl
Calories: 80
Fat: 7.4

Carbohydrates: 1.2
Proteins: 1.2

Low-carbohydrate Chinese chicken salad

Cooking time: 20 mins
Total time: 30 mins

INGREDIENTS

- 300 gr white cabbage, cut
- 200 gr Chinese cabbage, chopped
- 500 gr chicken fillet
- 4 cups of water
- 1/2 tsp garlic powder
- 1/2 tsp onion powder
- 1/4 tsp salt
- 20 ml soy sauce with less salt
- 3/4 cucumber
- 4 stalks of spring onion
- 150 gr radishes
- 2 tbsp sesame seeds
- bottle of Ready-to-use Oriental dressing (Jean Baton)
- 2 handfuls of fresh parsley, finely chopped

PREPARATION METHOD

In a big skillet, warm 4 cups of water, soy sauce, garlic powder, and onion powder. Stir briefly and then add the chook breasts to the pan. Bring the contents of the pan to the boil and simmer for 15-20 minutes with the lid at the pan.

Meanwhile, cut the cucumber, radishes, and spring onion into pieces. After 15-20 minutes of simmering, remove the skillet from the heat and place the chook breasts on a plate. Using a fork and knife, pull the chicken breasts aside into small portions.

Divide the Chinese cabbage, white cabbage, and chopped greens amongst 5 plates and area a little shredded chicken on top of every vegetable plate. Garnish with sesame seeds, parsley, and the Oriental salad dressing. Enjoy your meal!

NUTRITIONAL VALUES

Serving Size: 1/5
Calories: 187
Fats: 5.0

Carbohydrates: 6.0
Proteins: 26.2

Low-carbohydrate flaxseed buns

Cooking time: 15 mins
Total time: 25 mins

INGREDIENTS

- 80 gr linseed, broken
- 2 - 3 medium eggs
- 55 g grated Parmesan cheese

PREPARATION METHOD

1. Preheat the oven to one hundred eighty ° C. In a large bowl, mix all elements properly. Divide the batter into 6 equally sized dough balls.
2. Place a piece of baking paper on a baking tray and region the 6 balls of dough on it. Flatten the dough balls with the lower back of a spoon and shape them right into a round bun.
3. Bake the flaxseed buns inside the preheated oven for 10-12 mins. Let the rolls cool down after baking. Top the sandwiches along with your favored low-carbohydrate sandwich spread

NUTRITIONAL VALUES

Serving Size: 2 sandwiches
Calories: 223
Fat: 17.2
Carbohydrates: 2.3
Proteins: 15.1

Low-carbohydrate sushi

INGREDIENTS

- 2 nori sheets
- 1 ripe avocado
- 1/2 red bell pepper
- 1/4 carrot
- 1/4 cucumber
- 15 gr alfafa
- 1/4 red onion
- 1 tbsp sesame seeds
- soy sauce to taste

PREPARATION METHOD

1. Place the two nori sheets on a flat floor, worktop, or cutting board. Peel and reduce the avocado into cubes and put the cubes in a bowl. Then mash these cubes inside the bowl with a fork and set the bowl apart. Cut all of the greens into skinny strips and set this aside for a while.

2. Spread the avocado puree calmly on the lowest of both nori sheets. Carefully vicinity the thin strips of greens horizontally above the avocado puree on the nori sheets. Then take the lowest of the nori sheets and fold it over to the top of the filling, in the meantime keep the filling in an area with your hands and roll tightly until the end of the sheet. When you reach the end of the sheet, moist your index finger and roll the final piece. Then moisten your palms and rub the nori sheets. Wetting guarantees that the nori sheets stick collectively.

3. You can now cut the sushi rolls right into a preferred variety of portions with a pointy knife, but it is also viable to devour the roll like this. Garnish with the sesame seeds and serve with soy sauce. Enjoy your meal!

NUTRITIONAL VALUES

Serving Size: 1 roll
Calories: 201
Fats: 17.9

Carbohydrates: 6.0
Proteins: 4.1

Avocado tuna salad

Cooking time: 15 mins
Total time: 15 mins

INGREDIENTS

- 1 avocado
- lemon juice from 1 lemon
- 1/4 red onion, chopped
- 2 celery stalks, finely chopped
- 1 can of tuna in water
- salt and black pepper to taste

PREPARATION METHOD

1. Cut the avocado in 1/2 the usage of a knife. You do that by means of making a reduce lengthwise across the wick. Then turn the avocado along with your hands to loosen it. Then insert a pointy knife into the pit and lightly pull it out of the avocado 1/2.
2. Then spoon the pulp out of the avocado and keep the pores and skin. Mash the pulp in a bowl and add the red onion, celery, lemon juice, and herbs. Stir nicely after which add the drained tuna and blend well once more.
3. Return the avocado tuna salad to the avocado or location on a toasted low-carb sandwich. Enjoy your meal!

NUTRITIONAL VALUES

Serving Size: 1 portion
Calories: 304
Fat: 20.7

Carbohydrates: 4.4
Fiber: 6.9
Proteins: 21.6

Low-carbohydrate sandwich

Cooking time: 30 mins
Total time: 30 mins

INGREDIENTS

- 1 small cauliflower
- 1 large egg (L)
- 50 gr grated mozzarella
- 1/2 tsp salt
- 1/4 tsp black pepper
- extra spices to taste
- 1 tbsp butter
- 70 g spicy grated cheddar

PREPARATION METHOD

1. Place an oven rack in the oven after which preheat the oven to 220 degree. Take a sheet of parchment paper and grease the sheet with some olive oil.

2. Now take the small cauliflower and dispose of the leaves and black spots. Cut the cauliflower in 1/2 and cast off the stump. Cut what's left into small florets. Put the florets in a food processor or blender and turn it on until small rice grains form. Repeat this until you've got made rice from all of the florets. Are you short on time? Then use geared up-to-consume cauliflower rice

3. Heat and tbsp olive oil in a frying pan. Add the cauliflower rice to the pan and fry it inside four-five minutes. Let the rice calm down after baking and then add it to a smooth kitchen towel. Then wring out all of the moisture from the rice.

4. Place the dry rice in a large bowl and upload the grated mozzarella, egg, salt, and pepper. Add extra spices if favored. Mix the whole thing well inside the bowl with a whisk. Divide the batter over the baking paper and form 4 identical-sized squares. Bake the buns for 16 minutes till golden brown. Let cool for at least 10 mins after which cautiously remove the rolls from the baking paper with a cheese slicer.

5. Now grease one facet of each sandwich with butter. Heat a frying pan over medium heat and positioned the bun within the pan with the butter facet. Add shredded cheddar to the bun and put one bun on the pinnacle with the butter side up. Lower the heat and cook dinner for 2-4 minutes on every side, until the cheese has melted. Repeat with the alternative sandwiches!

NUTRITIONAL VALUES

Serving Size: 1 toasted sandwich
Calories: 343
Fats: 25.2

Carbohydrates: 6.0
Proteins: 21.3

Courgetti with chicken and pesto

Cooking time: 10 mins
Total time: 25 mins

INGREDIENTS

500 gr broccoli

- 400 gr chicken fillet à la minute
- 600 gr zucchini spaghetti
- 70 gr pesto alla Genovese
- 80 gr cherry tomatoes
- 30 gr pine nuts
- 75 gr arugula
- 50 gr grated Parmesan cheese
- 3 tbsp olive oil
- salt and pepper to taste
- optional: tablespoon of Crème fraîche

PREPARATION METHOD

1. Cut the broccoli into florets. Cook the broccoli in boiling water for 6-8 mins until tender. Meanwhile, season the chicken fillet together with your preferred spice blend. Place the bird breast in a greased frying pan and fry the fillets over medium warmness for five-6 minutes.
2. Cut the chicken fillet into cubes after baking. When the broccoli florets are cooked, drain the excess water from the pan.
3. Now heat 2 tbsp olive oil inside the frying pan and add the zucchini spaghetti. Fry the zucchini for 2 minutes after which upload the pesto, broccoli, and chicken. Stir properly and fry for any other 2-3 minutes, till everything within the pan is warm.
4. Divide the contents of the pan among four plates and garnish with pine nuts, Parmesan cheese, cherry tomatoes, and arugula. Enjoy your meal!

NUTRITIONAL VALUES

Serving Size: ¼
Calories: 356
Fats: 19.8
Carbohydrates: 8.9
Proteins: 36.3

Low-carbohydrate detox salad

Cooking time: 25 mins
Total time: 30 mins

INGREDIENTS

- 500 gr raw beets
- 4 carrots or 150 gr raw vegetables carrot julienne
- 100 gr arugula
- 100 gr feta cheese
- 25 ml olive oil
- 15 ml apple cider vinegar

PREPARATION METHOD

1. Take a big slicing board and reduce the ends of the beets away on it. Then peel the beets with a vegetable peeler and reduce a thin slice off the pinnacle and backside if essential. Then rinse the tuber beneath the tap.
2. Now take a huge container and grate all the beets finely above the box. Do the equal with the 4 carrots. Now take four plates and spread the arugula lightly. Add the grated carrot and beets and garnish with the feta cheese.
3. To make the dressing, placed the olive oil and apple cider vinegar in a box and blend nicely. Drizzle the dressing over the detox salad! Enjoy your meal

NUTRITIONAL VALUES

Serving Size: 1 portion
Calories: 168
Fats: 10.3

Carbohydrates: 9.9
Proteins: 6.9

Scrambled eggs with zucchini and shiitake

Cooking time: 10 mins
Total time: 25 mins

INGREDIENTS

- 4 medium eggs
- 1/2 medium zucchini
- 1 small onion
- 40 gr shiitake or chestnut mushrooms
- pepper and salt to taste
- 1 tbsp olive oil
- 1 slice of cheese
- salt and pepper to taste
- optional: clove of garlic

PREPARATION METHOD

1. Grab a massive cutting board and cut the zucchini, onion, and shiitake into small portions. Heat the olive oil in a frying pan over medium warmth. Add the sliced onions and fry for two mins. Add the zucchini and mushrooms and stir fry for 5 minutes extra.
2. Beat the eggs in a bowl and add salt and pepper to flavor. Add the eggs and a slice of cheese to the frying pan and fry with a wood spatula at the same time as stirring. Divide the scrambled eggs over 2 plates and revel in!

NUTRITIONAL VALUES

Serving Size: 1/2 of the scrambled eggs
Calories: 284
Fats: 19.0

Carbohydrates: 8.5
Proteins: 17.5

Low-carbohydrate sausage rolls

Cooking time: 20 mins
Total time: 40 mins

INGREDIENTS

- 4 unox hot dogs
- 120 gr grated mozzarella
- 75 gr almond flour
- 1 tsp xanthan gum
- 2 tbsp cream cheese
- 2 medium eggs
- 4 tbsp seeds & kernels mix (sesame seeds, poppy seeds, linseed)
- 1 - 2 tsp onion powder
- 1 tsp garlic powder

PREPARATION METHOD

1. Place the mozzarella and cream cheese in a microwave-safe bowl and warm within the microwave for 1.5 mins, till the cheese has melted. Mix nicely and set aside.
2. Then preheat the oven to 200 degree. In another bowl, blend the almond flour, 1 egg, and the xanthan gum. Add the cheese mixture to the flour aggregate and knead with wet hands into a lump-loose batter.
3. Shape the dough into four equal-sized balls and vicinity them on a baking tray lined with parchment paper. Carefully roll out each ball with moist palms until it's far approximately 40 cm lengthy.
4. Then wrap each piece of dough tightly around a warm canine and briefly put them on a plate. Then beat the last egg in a bowl with a whisk and spread it over the hot dogs with a brush. Then mix all of the seeds and spices in a bowl and dip the recent puppies inside the spice mixture.
5. Return the new puppies to the baking tray and bake them in the preheated oven till golden brown for 20 mins. Enjoy your meal!

NUTRITIONAL VALUES

Serving Size: 1 hot dog
Calories: 342
Fats: 27.2

Carbohydrates: 4.7
Proteins: 19.5

Low-carbohydrate caprese salad

Cooking time: 20 mins
Total time: 25 mins

INGREDIENTS

- 100 ml balsamic vinegar
- 1 tbsp olive oil
- 2 pieces of chicken fillet (300 gr)
- salt and fresh black pepper
- 200 gr chopped romaine salad
- 150 gr mini mozzarella balls
- 200 gr cherry tomatoes
- 1 avocado, cut into cubes
- handful of basil, finely chopped

PREPARATION METHOD

1. Put the balsamic vinegar in a saucepan and heat over medium warmness. Bring to a light boil and cook dinner for 4-6 minutes, until 50% of the balsamic vinegar has evaporated. Put the closing balsamic vinegar in a container and let it calm down.
2. Heat a tablespoon of olive oil in a skillet over medium warmth. Season the bird breasts with salt and pepper and region in a frying pan. Fry the chook breasts for 4 minutes on every side. Cut the hen breasts into cubes and allow them to calm down.
3. Place the romaine salad in a big bowl and upload the bird, mozzarella, cherry tomatoes, avocado, and basil. Garnish with the balsamic vinegar and divide into 2 quantities.

NUTRITIONAL VALUES

Serving Size: ½

Calories: 475

Fats: 26.0

Carbohydrates: 7.5

Proteins: 50.5

Lettuce wraps filled with turkey fillet and bacon

Cooking time: 10 mins
Total time: 15 mins

INGREDIENTS
Basil Mayonnaise:

- 2 - 3 tbsp mayonnaise
- 6 basil leaves
- optional: 1 small clove of garlic, crushed
- 1 tsp lemon juice

Wraps:

- 1 head of iceberg lettuce
- 6 slices of turkey or chicken fillet
- 4 slices of fried bacon
- 1 small avocado
- 1 Roma tomato
- salt and pepper to taste

PREPARATION METHOD

1. To make the basil mayonnaise, vicinity the mayonnaise, basil, finely overwhelmed garlic, and lemon juice in a small meal processor or blender. Switch at the tool, in brief, to combine the entirety well.
2. Then reduce the avocado and tomato into slices on a large reducing board. Grab the top of iceberg lettuce and tear off the two largest leaves. Put slices of hen or turkey breast on each. Spread a bit of basil mayonnaise on the pinnacle of the fillet slices. On top of this sediment, place another slice of turkey or chicken breast, bacon, tomato slices, and avocado.
3. Season lightly with salt and pepper then fold the lowest of the lettuce wrap up, in the facets, and then roll it close like a burrito. Serve the lettuce wraps cold.

NUTRITIONAL VALUES

Serving Size: 1 wrap
Calories: 300
Fat: 27.5

Carbohydrates: 4.8
Proteins: 12.8

Low-carb cauliflower couscous

Cooking time: 10 mins   **Total time: 25 mins**

INGREDIENTS

- 600 gr cauliflower florets
- 75 gr sundried tomatoes
- 1 - 2 cloves of garlic, finely crushed
- 1 tbsp olive oil
- 150 gr leek, finely chopped
- salt and pepper to taste

- pinch of paprika
- pinch of finely ground cumin
- 1 tbsp lemon juice
- 50 gr walnuts, chopped into pieces
- optional: feta cheese to taste

PREPARATION METHOD

1. Grab a container with water and soak the sun-dried tomatoes in it. Then put the florets of cauliflower in a food processor and grind it granular, similar to real couscous. Add lemon juice to the cauliflower and season with salt, pepper, cumin, and paprika.
2. Grab a medium frying pan and heat a tablespoon of olive oil in it. Add the finely beaten cloves of garlic and the portions of leek and fry for a couple of minutes over medium warmth.
3. Meanwhile, grasp the box with sun-dried tomatoes and permit the water to drain. Then cut the sun-dried tomatoes into small pieces and upload them to the frying pan.
4. Then upload the cauliflower couscous and the walnuts to the pan and fry until executed. Be careful no longer to overcook it, due to the fact then it'll change into a porridge. Divide among four plates and enjoy!

NUTRITIONAL VALUES

Serving Size: ¼   Carbohydrates: 12.5

Calories: 230   Proteins: 5.4

Fat: 14.5

Greek salad of grilled halloumi

Cooking time: 10 mins   **Total time: 15 mins**

INGREDIENTS

- 225 gr halloumi cheese
- 100 gr salad mix of your choice
- 1 cucumber
- 150 cherry tomatoes
- 4 stalks of spring onion

- 1 avocado
- juice of 1 lemon
- 2 tbsp olive oil
- 1 tbsp balsamic vinegar

PREPARATION METHOD

Grab a large reducing board and cut the spring onion, cherry tomatoes, and cucumber into small pieces on it. Then take the avocado and reduce it in half. Then take away the pit and peel and additionally cut the avocado into small pieces. Put the salad, cucumber, cherry tomatoes, spring onion, avocado in a big bowl and blend the whole lot collectively.

Now take a small bowl and blend in the lemon juice, olive oil, and balsamic vinegar, and set it apart. Then cut the halloumi into frivolously sized slices and location on a hot grill. Grill until the halloumi slices flip brown.

Divide the salad from the bowl over 3 plates and serve with some slices of halloumi and the dressing. Enjoy your meal!

NUTRITIONAL VALUES

Serving Size: 1/3   Carbohydrates: 8.1

Calories: 318   Proteins: 17.6

Fats: 24.1

Vitello tonnato

Cooking time: 10 mins   **Total time: 15 mins**

INGREDIENTS

- 185 gr tuna in canned water
- 3 tbsp mayonnaise
- 3 tbsp capers
- lemon juice to taste

- 75 gr arugula
- 200 gr fricandeau
- 50 gr cherry tomatoes

PREPARATION METHOD

1. Divide the fricandeau over two plates. Puree the tuna and mayonnaise with the hand blender. Season with lemon juice, pepper, and salt if desired. Divide the tuna aggregate over the fricandeau and eventually placed the arugula, capers, and tomato over the Vitello tomato.

NUTRITIONAL VALUES

Serving Size: ½   Carbohydrates: 1.6
Calories: 364   Proteins: 36.4
Fats: 22.6

Spicy Indian scrambled eggs with spinach

Cooking time: 15 mins
Total time: 25 mins

INGREDIENTS

- 1 - 2 tsp cumin seeds or cumin powder
- 1 - 2 tsp mustard seeds
- 1 onion, finely chopped
- 25 gr butter
- 1 tbsp olive oil
- 200 gr baby spinach
- 1 tsp garam masala seasoning
- 2 tsp turmeric
- 8 medium eggs
- 4 low- carb wraps
- 3 tsp finely chopped mint
- 6 tbsp yogurt
- salt and black pepper to taste

PREPARATION METHOD

2. Briefly toast the mustard and cumin seeds over low heat in a lightly greased pan. Use a deep frying pan as the seeds can pop up once they get warm. Meanwhile, cut the onion into small portions and upload it to the pan along with a tbsp of butter. Fry the onions until golden brown for approximately five mins. Then add the spinach and fry it till it has gotten smaller and set apart.
3. Then take any other pan and heat the rest of the butter and a little olive oil in it. Add the garam masala and turmeric and cook for 1-2 mins. Meanwhile, beat the eggs in a massive bowl. Add the eggs to the pan and fry whilst stirring.
4. Meanwhile, warmth the wraps inside the oven or in a frying pan. Then take the spinach from the set aside pan and reduce it into small portions and dispose of any extra liquid using a sieve. Add the spinach to the scrambled eggs and prepare dinner for more mins.
5. In-between, reduce the mint into small pieces and upload this to the yogurt in a field. Serve the scrambled eggs with the wrap and yogurt sauce.

NUTRITIONAL VALUES

Serving Size: ¼

Calories: 230

Fats: 15.8

Carbohydrates: 6.1

Proteins: 14.5

Creamy cauliflower risotto

Cooking time: 10 mins
Total time: 15 mins

INGREDIENTS

- 400 gr of cauliflower rice
- 33 gr mascarpone
- 2 tbsp butter
- 25 gr green pesto
- 2 tbsp grated Parmesan cheese
- 1/2 tsp salt
- 1/4 tsp garlic powder
- 1/4 tsp black pepper

PREPARATION METHOD

1. Heat a tablespoon of butter in a large frying pan or wok pan. Add the cauliflower rice to the pan and fry for 3-4 minutes simultaneously as stirring.
2. Then upload the rest of the butter, mascarpone, and all the herbs and fry for 2 mins while stirring. Finally, add the Parmesan and fry for any other minute.
3. Let cool for 2 mins after adding the green pesto and stir it through the cauliflower risotto. Divide the risotto into portions and enjoy!

NUTRITIONAL VALUES

Serving Size: ½
Calories: 228
Fat: 18.9

Carbohydrates: 10.0
Proteins: 6.8

Adam's low-carb bread

Cooking time: 40 mins   **Total time: 60 min**

INGREDIENTS

- 1 pack of Adam's bread mix white or brown
- 230 ml of lukewarm water

PREPARATION METHOD

1. In a huge bowl, add the bread blend and. Take a tumbler and fill it with 230 ml lukewarm water and add the yeast at the same time as stirring. Then add the yeast and water to the bread mix and knead it by hand for about two mins. Now take a cake tin and positioned the dough in it. Put the cake tin with the dough within the oven for forty-five minutes at 50 degrees so that it may rise properly.

2. When the bread has risen, take it out of the oven and sprinkle the pinnacle with a little water. Bake the bread when it has risen properly for some other 50 minutes within the preheated oven at two hundred degree. Let the bread cool at the counter for half an hour after baking. Cut the bread into thirteen slices and enjoy!

NUTRITIONAL VALUES

Serving Size: 1 slice (35 gr)

Calories: 82

Fats: 3.7

Carbohydrates: 0.2

Proteins: 11.2

APPETIZER

Low-carbohydrate sajoer beans

Cooking time: 15 mins
Total time: 25 mins

INGREDIENTS

- 500 gr green beans
- 1 onion
- 1 clove of garlic
- 2 cm fresh ginger
- 1 tsp laos herbs
- 2 to 3 tsp sambal oelek
- 1 tbsp olive oil
- 1 tsp soy sauce
- 200 ml coconut milk
- 1/2 vegetable stock cube

PREPARATION METHOD

1. Clean the green beans and cut the ends of the beans off. Add the green beans to a pan of boiling water and pre-prepare dinner for five-6 mins.
2. Meanwhile, add the onion, garlic, ginger, galangal, and sambal to a blender and mix right into a first-rate paste. After cooking, placed the beans in a colander and ensure that each extra liquid has tired.
3. Heat a tablespoon of olive oil in a frying pan and upload the spice paste to the pan. Then add the green beans and fry for 2-three mins while stirring. Then upload the coconut milk and soy sauce and collapse the stock dice over the pan.
4. Stew the green beans over a low warmth within 5-8 mins. Divide the beans among four plates and serve with cauliflower rice and rendang if desired.

NUTRITIONAL VALUES

Serving Size: 1 portion (1/3)   Fats: 14.8   Fiber: 7.5
Calories: 191   Carbohydrates: 5.8 Proteins: 5.3

Fresh cucumber salad

Cooking time: 10 mins   **Total time: 10 mins**

INGREDIENTS

- 2 cucumbers
- 1/2 red onion
- 125 gr Greek yogurt
- 1 tbsp white wine vinegar
- 1 tbsp fresh dill, finely chopped
- 1/4 tsp salt
- 1/4 tsp garlic powder

PREPARATION METHOD.

1. Clean the cucumber and reduce it into thin slices with a cheese slicer or a sharp knife. Then cut the crimson onion into earrings and upload it to a large bowl along with the cucumber.
2. In every other bowl, mix the Greek yogurt with the white wine vinegar, sliced dill, salt, and garlic powder. Add the dressing to the cucumber salad and mix well.
3. Divide the cucumber salad over 4 plates and garnish with more dill or red onion if desired. Enjoy your meal!

NUTRITIONAL VALUES

Serving Size: 1 portion (1/4   Fats: 3.8   Proteins: 2.7

Calories: 67   Carbohydrates: 4.4

Cauliflower salad with cheese

Cooking time: 15 mins
Total time: 25 mins

INGREDIENTS

cauliflowers lade

- 400 gr cauliflower
- 1 red pepper
- 200 gr sliced red cabbage (fresh)
- 2 stalks of celery
- 2 stalks of spring onion
- 100 gr cheese cubes or feta

Dressing

- 4 tbsp olive oil
- lemon juice from 1/2 lemon
- handful of basil finely chopped

PREPARATION METHOD

1. Cut the cauliflower into florets and cook the florets al dente for approximately five-eight mins. It is likewise viable to roast the cauliflower. To do that, drizzle the cauliflower with olive oil and bake the florets at two hundred degrees for 15-20 mins.
2. Meanwhile, reduce the bell pepper, celery, and spring onion into small portions. Add this to a bowl and blend nicely. Nowcast off the cauliflower from the oven or pan and allow the excess moisture to drain. Let the cauliflower cool down for some time, and then season with salt and pepper.
3. Add the cold cauliflower to the bowl with the opposite vegetables and blend properly again. Now make the dressing by blending the olive oil, lemon juice, and basil in a small bowl.
4. Divide the salad among three plates. Finally, reduce the cheese cubes into even smaller cubes and serve the salad with the dressing and cheese cubes. Enjoy your meal!

NUTRITIONAL VALUES

Serving size: 1/3 of the total
Calories: 268

Fats: 19.8
Carbohydrates: 7.8

Fiber: 5.8
Proteins: 12.1

Fresh green salad

Cooking time: 10 mins
Total time: 10 mins

INGREDIENTS

Salad:

- 150 gr salad mix
- 1 cucumber
- 125 gr cherry tomatoes
- 1/2 red onion
- 100 gr radishes
- handful of pine nuts
- handful of sunflower seeds

Dressing:

- 35 ml olive oil
- 1 tbsp lemon juice
- 1/2 tbsp vinegar
- 1 tsp mustard
- 1/2 tsp garlic powder
- salt and pepper to taste

PREPARATION METHOD

1. Quarter the cucumber and cherry tomatoes. Then take the radishes and smooth them. Cut the radishes into thin slices and set them apart. Then peel the onion and cut it into thin rings.
2. Mix all of the French dressing substances in a bowl with a whisk.
3. Divide the lettuce blend over 4 plates and garnish the plates with the pieces of cucumber, tomato, radish, onion, pine nuts, and sunflower seeds. Serve the salad with the French dressing. Enjoy your meal!

NUTRITIONAL VALUES

Serving Size: 1/4 of the salad   Fats: 12.4   Proteins: 3.6
Calories: 148   Carbohydrates: 4.3

Rutabaga fries

Cooking time: 30 mins
Total time: 35 mins

INGREDIENTS

- 400 gr turnips
- 2 tbsp olive oil
- 1 tsp cayenne pepper
- 1 tsp paprika powder
- 1/2 tsp garlic powder
- salt and pepper to taste
- optional: fries herbs

PREPARATION METHOD

1. Peel the kohlrabi cut them into small fries, or use ready-made kohlrabi fries. Fill a pan with salted water and bring it to a boil. Add the turnip fries to the pan and cook for three-5 mins.
2. After cooking, pour the contents of the pan right into a colander and allow the excess liquid to drain nicely. Then pat the swede fries dry with a paper towel. Place the fries on a baking tray coated with parchment paper and add the olive oil and herbs. Mix the whole lot properly with your palms so that the herbs and oil are frivolously disbursed.
3. For preparation in the oven: preheat the oven to two hundred ranges. Place the baking tray within the oven and bake the turnip fries for 25-half-hour within the preheated oven.
4. For education inside the air fryer: preheat the air fryer at one hundred eighty degree. Put the turnip fries inside the basket and bake for 12 mins at a hundred and eighty degree. Then increase the temperature to 2 hundred ranges and bake for another 5 minutes for a crispy layer. Serve the fries with sugar-loose ketchup and mayonnaise. Enjoy your meal!

NUTRITIONAL VALUES

Serving size: 1/2 of the total
Calories: 110

Fat: 9.2
Carbohydrates: 4.0

Proteins: 2.0

Green asparagus with Parma ham

Cooking time: 10 mins
Total time: 15 mins

INGREDIENTS

- 400 gr green asparagus
- 100 gr Prosciutto di Parma (Parma ham)
- 40 g grated parmesan cheese
- 1 - 2 tbsp olive oil
- salt and pepper to taste
- lemon juice to taste (optional)

PREPARATION METHOD

1. Preheat the convection oven to two hundred degree and line a baking tray with a parchment paper sheet. Clean the asparagus with touch water and reduce away the difficult ends.
2. Then cut the slices of Parma ham in half. Sprinkle the slices of Parma ham with a touch of grated parmesan cheese. Then wrap a slice of Parma ham with parmesan cheese tightly around one asparagus and repeat until all of the asparagus has a slice of ham.
3. Then region the asparagus at the baking tray and sprinkle with the last grated parmesan cheese, and drizzle with the olive oil. Finally, season the asparagus with a little salt and pepper.
4. Bake the asparagus inside the preheated oven for eight-10 minutes. The asparagus is finished if they bend slightly while picked up. After frying, divide asparagus into four quantities and serve with a balsamic sauce if favored. Enjoy your meal!

NUTRITIONAL VALUES

Serving size: 1/4 of the total
Calories: 161

Fat: 11.3
Carbohydrates: 3.3

Fiber: 1.5
Proteins: 11.0

Casserole with green beans

Cooking time: 20 mins
Total time: 35 mins

INGREDIENTS

- 600 gr green beans
- 250 gr mushrooms
- 125 gr bacon strips
- 2 shallots, finely chopped
- 250 ml of cooking cream
- 50 gr cream cheese
- 30 g grated parmesan cheese
- salt and pepper to taste
- optional: cayenne pepper to taste

PREPARATION METHOD

1. Preheat the oven to 180 degree. Then reduce the mushrooms into slices and the onion into small cubes. Then take a massive frying pan and fry the bacon in it until tender and crispy. After frying, put the bacon in a bowl and blot away the excess fats.
2. Fry the chopped onion and mushrooms in the equal frying pan over medium warmth within approx. Three minutes. Then add the cooking cream, cream cheese, and herbs to the pan. Bring this to the boil while stirring and preparing dinner for about four minutes, till the sauce starts to thicken. Then lower the warmth and simmer for any other 6-eight minutes to thicken the sauce further.
3. Meanwhile, grab a massive pan and fill it with water. Add the green beans and a pinch of salt to the pan and cook dinner the green beans for about 8-10 minutes until al dente. After cooking, drain the green beans properly and pat dry with a paper towel if necessary.
4. Then add the cooked green beans to the pan with the mushroom sauce and blend well with a spatula. Spoon the pan's contents into an oven dish and bake for 15 mins in the preheated oven.
5. After 15 mins, dispose of the dish from the oven and sprinkle with the fried bacon and parmesan cheese. Then go back the casserole to the oven and bake for another 5 minutes. Divide into four portions after baking. Enjoy your meal!

NUTRITIONAL VALUES

Serving Size: 1/4 of the dish
Calories: 260

Fats: 18.1
Carbohydrates: 11.8

Fiber: 7.2
Proteins: 10.0

Sugar snaps from the oven

Cooking time: 10 mins   **Total time: 15 mins**

INGREDIENTS

- 225 gr sugar snaps
- 40 gr grated Parmesan cheese
- 15 ml of olive oil
- 15 g shallots, cut into pieces
- 1 tsp fresh thyme, chopped into pieces
- salt and pepper to taste

PREPARATION METHOD.

1. Preheat the oven to 225 ranges. Then take the sparkling sugar snaps and get rid of the ends and any threads. Spread the sugar snaps on a baking tray covered with parchment paper and brush the sugar snaps with olive oil. Then sprinkle the Parmesan cheese shallots, thyme, and sea salt over the sugar snaps.
2. Bake the sugar snaps within the preheated oven for 6-10 minutes. Divide into 4 equal portions and serve!

NUTRITIONAL VALUES

Serving Size: ¼   Fats: 6.2   Proteins: 5.0

Calories: 93   Carbohydrates: 3.6

cauliflower Purée

Cooking time: 10 mins   **Total time: 18 mins**

INGREDIENTS

- 1 medium cauliflower
- 2 - 3 tsp finely ground garlic
- 4 tbsp butter
- 1/2 tsp salt
- 1/2 tsp pepper
- olive oil to taste

PREPARATION METHOD

1. Take the cauliflower and cut away all brown and black spots. Then cast off the cauliflower leaves and reduce the cauliflower into small pieces.
2. Boil or steam the cauliflower in a saucepan with water for approximately 10-15 minutes. After cooking, pour away the excess water using a lid or colander. Then put the cauliflower, butter, garlic, and other herbs in a large bowl and blend until easy with a hand blender. If you do not have a stick blender, you could additionally mix substances in a blender or meal processor. Divide into 4 quantities and serve! Garnish with a little olive oil and further clean black pepper if favored.

NUTRITIONAL VALUES

Serving Size: ¼   Fats: 12.4   Proteins: 2.9

Calories: 142   Carbohydrates: 8.0

Fried Brussels sprouts with pecans

Cooking time: 10 mins   **Total time: 20 mins**

INGREDIENTS

- 350 gr Brussels sprouts
- 40 gr pecans
- 20 gr dried dates

- 2 tbsp olive oil
- 1 tsp apple cider vinegar
- 1 tsp mustard

- 1 tbsp butter

PREPARATION METHOD

1. Clean the Brussels sprouts and blanch them in boiling water for 3 minutes. Meanwhile, cut the pecans in half and, in short, toast them in a dry frying pan.
2. In a small bowl, combine the olive oil, apple cider vinegar, mustard, salt, and pepper. Drain the Brussels sprouts and rinse with cold water. Then warmness a tablespoon of butter in a frying pan and fry the Brussels sprouts for three to four minutes until al dente.
3. Meanwhile, reduce the dates into small portions. Cut the Brussels sprouts in half after baking. In a huge bowl, blend the Brussels sprouts with the nuts and fruits and warm the whole thing up a bit longer. Pour the dressing over the Brussels sprouts and enjoy!

NUTRITIONAL VALUES

Serving Size: 1/3   Fats: 18.6   Proteins: 5.8
Calories: 239   Carbohydrates: 8.6

Low-carb fries

Cooking time: 20 mins   **Total time: 40 mins**

INGREDIENTS

- 1/2 celeriac
- 1 tbsp olive oil
- 1 tsp paprika powder
- 1/2 tsp salt
- 1/4 tsp black pepper

PREPARATION METHOD

1. Preheat an oven to 205 ranges. Take the celeriac and put off the skin and cut the flesh into very thin fries. Put the fries in a bowl and blend with the herbs and olive oil.
2. Then take a baking tray coated with parchment paper and spread the fries frivolously at the baking tray. Bake the fries for 20 to 40 mins inside the preheated oven (relies upon the thickness of the fries), shaking on occasion while baking. Serve with a sauce and experience!

NUTRITIONAL VALUES

Serving Size: 1/3   Fats: 4.0   Proteins: 1.0

Calories: 47   Carbohydrates: 3.0

DESSERT AND SNACKS

Low-carb New York cheesecake

Cooking time: 20 mins
Total time: 80 mins

INGREDIENTS

- Bottom
- 150 gr almond flour
- 25 gr coconut flour
- 75 gr butter, melted
- 30 g erythritol
- 1/4 tsp salt
- Stuffing
- 225 gr mascarpone
- 250 gr cream cheese
- 40 gr erythritol
- 3 eggs (M)
- 1 tsp vanilla extract
- 15 gr Steviala Sweet & Vanilla
- optional: 3 g gelatin powder

PREPARATION METHOD

1. Preheat the convection oven to one hundred seventy degree. Add all the backside substances to a mixing bowl and mix or knead into a smooth batter. Cover a cake tin or springform pan (24 cm) with a baking paper sheet.
2. Bake the bottom for approx.—15 to twenty minutes inside the preheated oven. The bottom is prepared whilst it has a pleasing golden-brown shade. Let the lowest cool out of doors the oven.
3. Now lower the oven temperature to 150 degrees. Grab a huge bowl and upload all of the ingredients for the filling. Then beat this for approx. 2 mins with an electric mixer till creamy. Then divide the filling over the cooled bottom.
4. Place an oven dish or baking tray filled with two hundred ml of water at the bottom of the oven. Now vicinity the spring shape in the oven's middle on a rack. Bake the cheesecake for 60 mins inside the preheated oven (150 degree).
5. When the cheesecake is ready, turn off the oven and go away the oven door ajar. Let the cheesecake cool to room temperature, after which positioned inside the fridge for approximately 4 to six hours. Or preferably the entire nighttime. Cut .. Into pieces and experience!

NUTRITIONAL VALUES

Serving Size: 1 slice (1/12)   Fat: 24.9   Proteins: 6.5

Calories: 264   Carbohydrates: 2.3

Low-carbohydrate cake roll with strawberries

11.

Cooking time: 50 mins   **Total time: 65 mins**

INGREDIENTS

- Cake roll
- 4 eggs (M)
- 60 gr almond flour
- 20 gr erythritol
- 4 grams of baking powder
- 1 tsp vanilla extract
- Strawberry jelly
- 200 gr strawberries
- 2 tbsp water
- 1/4 tsp lemon juice

- 10 g erythritol
- 1 gelatin sheet
- Whipped cream filling

- 150 gr whipped cream
- 100 gr MonChou cream cheese
- 20 gr erythritol
- Topping (optional)
- 50 gr sugar-free white chocolate
- 50 gr sugar-free milk chocolate
- 1/2 tsp vanilla extract

PREPARATION METHOD.

1. Strawberry jam. Soak the gelatin sheet in cold water for 10 mins. Then upload the strawberries, water, lemon juice, and erythritol to a saucepan. Put this at the hearth and allow it to boil for about five minutes, even as stirring. Then squeeze out the gelatin sheet and upload it simultaneously as stirring until it has melted. Then use a fork to press the strawberries to the favored thickness. Spoon the strawberry jam into a bowl and allow it to cool down.

2. Cake roll. Preheat the convection oven to 180 degree. Then you put a baking tray (forty × 40 cm) equipped with a bit of baking paper. Split 2 eggs. Then upload the egg whites with the erythritol to a big mixing bowl. Beat the egg whites with an electric mixer and set them apart.

3. Now take a brand new bowl and add the final 2 eggs, egg yolks, vanilla extract, almond flour, and baking powder. Mix this with a whisk to a smooth batter. Then spatula lightly through the egg whites. Spoon the batter onto the baking paper. Spread this out lightly, approximately 1 cm thick, and bake for 12 minutes within the preheated oven.

4. Whipped cream filling. Prepare the whipped cream filling while baking. To do this, upload the whipped cream, monchou cream cheese, and erythritol to a bowl and beat with an electric mixer until creamy.

5. Cake roll. Remove the cake from the oven after baking. Place a bit of parchment paper on your counter. Now take the cake and flip it over on a baking paper sheet. Remove the top sheet, cover the cake with the strawberry jam, and then the whipped cream filling. Now roll the cake tightly together with your palms and wrap the roll with household pores and skin foil. Place inside the fridge and permit it set for a minimum of 30 minutes.

6. Topping. Melt the chocolate au-bain-marie in a heat-resistant bowl over a saucepan with water. Divide the chocolate over the cake roll with a spoon. Cut the cake roll into approx. 13 slices. Store the cake roll within the fridge or keep with the slice within the freezer. Enjoy your meal!

NUTRITIONAL VALUES

Serving Size: 1 slice (1/13) without chocolate

Calories: 114
Fats: 10.1

Carbohydrates: 1.6
Proteins: 3.5

White chocolate mousse with raspberries

Cooking time: 10 mins
Total time: 90 mins

INGREDIENTS

- Mousse
- 125 ml of whipped cream
- 1 egg (m)
- 1/2 sheet of gelatin
- 30 g erythritol
- 75 gr white chocolate , sugar free
- Raspberry jelly:
- 100 gr raspberries
- 1/2 sheet of gelatin
- 20 gr erythritol

Topping

- raspberries as desired
- blueberries as desired
- grated white chocolate

PREPARATION METHOD.

1. Please start with the raspberry jelly to chill in the mousse's preparation course. Soak the gelatin in cold water and add the raspberries and erythritol to a saucepan. Bring this to a boil.
2. Pour the boiling jelly through a sieve right into a box. Press the sieve nicely with a spoon to simplest the seeds remain. Add the gelatin to the jelly while stirring. Set the jelly aside and keep with the mousse
3. Also, for the mousse, soak the gelatin in cold water. Then beat the whipped cream with an electric-powered mixer in a large mixing bowl. Now take saucepans and position them at the fireplace with a water layer.
4. Place heat-resistant bowls on the pinnacle of the two saucepans. Add the white chocolate to at least one bowl and the egg and erythritol to the alternative. Melt the chocolate and beat the egg creamy and fluffy with a whisk. Then put off the dish with the egg from the saucepan and upload the gelatin simultaneously as stirring.
5. Now grasp an electric-powered mixer and maintain beating until the egg mixture is at room temperature. Then cautiously fold the melted white chocolate into the egg aggregate and, sooner or later, the whipped cream.
6. Spread some culmination and raspberry jelly on the lowest of the glasses. Then divide 1/2 of the white chocolate mousse over the four glasses. Add some raspberry jelly and the last chocolate mousse. Top it off with a layer of raspberry jelly and a few fruits.
7. Put the dishes within the fridge for at least 1 hour earlier than serving. The longer the mousse is within the refrigerator, the stiffer it turns into.

NUTRITIONAL VALUES

Serving Size: 1 bowl (1/4)

Calories: 225

Fats: 18.6

Carbohydrates: 4.9

Proteins: 3.5

Low-carbohydrate eton mess

Cooking time: 45 mins
Total time: 75 mins

INGREDIENTS

- meringues
- 2 proteins (M)
- 25 g erythritol
- pinch of salt
- Forest fruit sauce
- 40 gr strawberries
- 20 gr raspberries
- 15 ml of water
- 10 g erythritol

Stuffing

- 200 ml whipped cream, 35% fat
- 100 gr mascarpone
- 1 tsp vanilla extract
- 40 gr erythritol

Topping:

- 50 gr raspberries
- 60 gr strawberries
- 50 gr blueberries
- 50 gr blackberries
- optional: fresh mint

PREPARATION METHOD

1. Preheat the convection oven to 140 degree. Split the eggs and upload the egg whites together with the erythritol and a pinch of salt to a mixing bowl. Beat the egg whites with an electric mixer within approx. 3 mins.
2. Then scoop the beaten egg whites with a spoon onto a baking tray covered with parchment paper. Spread the egg whites to an excellent thickness and bake for forty-five minutes in the preheated oven. Let the froth settle down after baking.
3. Meanwhile, make the wooded area fruit sauce to add all of the substances for the sauce to a pan. Place the pan on medium warmth and produce the fruits to a boil. Let it simmer for 2 mins while stirring. Then flip off the heat and let it cool to room temperature. Use a hand blender to make a clean sauce from the result.
4. Now take a new bowl and add all of the filling ingredients. Beat the whole lot with an electric-powered mixer until mild and stiff. After beating, put the filling in the refrigerator.
5. Now fall apart the meringue and upload it to a bowl. Grab your dessert glasses and start constructing. Add a handful of meringues to the glass and placed a few fresh culmination on the pinnacle. Now add 2 tbsp whipped cream filling and a bit of the sauce. Repeat this till all of your elements are long past.
6. Decorate the glasses with clean mint is essential. Do no longer prepare the Eton mess until you serve it. The foam will become smooth in the fridge. Enjoy your meal!

NUTRITIONAL VALUES

Serving Size: 1 bowl (1/4)   Fats: 30.2   Proteins: 5.5
Calories: 317   Carbohydrates: 6.7

Low-carbohydrate mini tiramisu

Cooking time: 30 mins

Total time: 45 mins

INGREDIENTS

- Sponge base
- 35 gr almond flour
- 5 gr coconut flour
- 1/4 tsp baking powder
- 1 egg
- 1/2 tsp vanilla extract
- 1 tbsp whipped cream
- 25 g erythritol
- 50 gr ricotta
- 1 espresso

Stuffing

- 50 ml whipped cream
- 75 gr mascarpone
- 1 egg yolk
- 1/2 tsp vanilla extract
- 20 gr Steviala Frost
- cocoa powder to taste

PREPARATION method

1. Preheat the convection oven or air fryer to 175 degree. In a massive bowl, blend the almond flour, coconut flour, baking powder, and erythritol nicely collectively. Then upload the ricotta, whipped cream, vanilla extract, and egg to the bowl. Stir the contents of the bowl with a whisk till smooth.

2. Grease a large ramekin (12 cm) or small ramekins (7 cm) with a little butter or oil. Then divide the batter from the bowl flippantly between the two ramekins. Place the ramekins in the oven or air fryer and bake for approximately 20 minutes inside the air fryer or 25-30 minutes inside the oven. After 10 mins, cowl the ramekins with aluminum foil so that the pinnacle does now not turn brown.

3. Meanwhile, make the filling using whipping the whipped cream with an electric-powered mixer until stiff in a cold bowl. While beating, add the mascarpone, vanilla, erythritol, and egg yolk. Whisk until stiff peaks shape. Do not beat too lengthy, as this may create a better structure.

4. When the lowest has cooled, you may cautiously pour 1 brewed espresso over the two bottoms. Then spread the mascarpone filling over the bottoms and garnish with cocoa powder. Enjoy your meal!

NUTRITIONAL VALUES

Serving Size: 1 bowl

Calories: 450

Fats: 42.3

Carbohydrates: 4.7

Proteins: 12.8

Low-carbohydrate strawberry flan

Cooking time: 30 mins   **Total time: 110 mins**

INGREDIENTS

- Bottom
- 200 gr almond flour
- 20 gr coconut flour
- 1 egg (M)
- 110 gr butter, unsalted
- 40 gr erythritol
- pinch of salt
- Custard

- 200 gr whipped cream
- 40 gr erythritol
- 3 egg yolks
- 1 tsp vanilla extract
- 2 gr gelatin powder

Topping

- 200 gr whipped cream
- 75 gr mascarpone

- 40 gr erythritol
- 1/2 tsp vanilla extract
- 300 gr strawberries
- optional: mint
- optional: almond flakes

PREPARATION METHOD.

1. Preheat the convection oven to 175 degree. In a massive bowl, combine all of the elements for the base. Then mix everything nicely along with your palms to shape a dough ball—grease a cake tin (25 cm) with butter, or line the tin with baking paper.
2. Divide the dough over the cake tin and make a raised facet. Then bake the bottom within the preheated oven for 25-30 minutes, until it's miles golden brown. Allow the lowest to cool completely after baking.
3. Meanwhile, make the pastry cream to add the egg yolks to a bowl at the side of a dash of whipped cream. Beat the yolks and set them aside. Then heat the last whipped cream in a small saucepan. When it's far heat, add the gelatin, vanilla, and erythritol whilst stirring, till the entirety is dissolved.
4. Now add the egg yolks with cream. Heat the pan's contents, even as stirring, until the cream has thickened. Turn off the heat and allow the pastry cream to cool to room temperature. Then add the cream to the cooled bottom and put it inside the fridge for approximately 1 hour.
5. Meanwhile, make the whipped cream topping using whipping cream, mascarpone, erythritol, and vanilla in a bowl until stiff. Remove the cake from the refrigerator and use a spatula to unfold the topping over the cake. Decorate the cake with strawberries and probably mint and almond shavings. Enjoy your meal!

NUTRITIONAL VALUES

Serving Size: 1 slice (1/12)   Fat: 28.2   Proteins: 6.8
Calories: 337   Carbohydrates: 4.3

Low-carbohydrate white chocolate cheesecake

Cooking time: 10 mins   **Total time: 300 mins**

INGREDIENTS

- Bottom
- 100 gr almond flour
- 60 gr melted butter
- 40 gr erythritol
- 1 egg yolk
- 2 tsp cinnamon
- 1 tsp gingerbread spices

Stuffing
- 225 gr mascarpone
- 200 ml whipped cream
- 150 gr monchou
- 150 gr white chocolate , sugar free
- 40 gr erythritol

- 15 gr gelatin powder

Topping
- 150 gr raspberries
- 3 tbsp water
- 5 gr gelatin powder
- optional: white chocolate
- optional: fresh fruit

PREPARATION METHOD

1. Preheat the convection oven to a hundred and seventy degrees. Then mix all of the bottom elements nicely in a large bowl. Line a springform pan (sixteen cm) with baking paper, both the bottom and aspects. Pour the batter into the tin and bake the lowest in the oven for about 30 minutes.

2. Meanwhile, in a huge bowl, beat the monchou and mascarpone fluffy with an electric mixer. Add the erythritol while mixing. Now take another bowl and whip one hundred fifty ml creamy cream in it until it has doubled in extent. Add the whipped cream to the monchou and mascarpone and whisk collectively.

3. Fill a saucepan with a layer of water. Bring the water to a boil and area a warmth-resistant bowl on the pan. Put the white chocolate in the bowl and melt the chocolate au-bain-marie. After melting, progressively stir the chocolate into the monchou mixture.

4. Meanwhile, warm the final 50 ml of whipped cream in a small pan. Add 15 grams of gelatin powder to the recent whipped cream whilst stirring. Be careful now not to permit the whipped cream to boil. Add the whipped cream with dissolved gelatin to the monchou combinations simultaneously as stirring.

5. Pour the monchou mixture into the spring shape with the cooled bottom and permit the cheesecake to set in the fridge for a minimum of three hours.

6. Start with the topping after 3 hours. To do that, puree the raspberries and add them to a saucepan. Add three tbsp water and switch on the warmth. Heat the raspberries over low heat and when the mixture is warm, add five g gelatin powder. Melt the powder and flip off the warmth.

7. Remove the cake from the refrigerator and pour the topping over it. Let the cake stiffen for another 2 hours, beautifying with white chocolate and sparkling fruit if necessary. Enjoy your meal!

NUTRITIONAL VALUES

Serving Size: 1 slice (1/12)   Fats: 30.1   Proteins: 4.7
Calories: 320   Carbohydrates: 4.0

Low-carbohydrate coconut pudding

Cooking time: 10 mins
Total time: 135 mins

INGREDIENTS

- 50 gr grated coconut
- 20 gr Steviala Crystal
- 50 gr cream cheese or dairy spread
- 1 egg, beaten
- 125 ml of whipped cream
- 150 ml coconut milk
- 1 tsp vanilla aroma

PREPARATION METHOD

1. In a microwave-safe bowl, mix 1/2 of the whipped cream with the grated coconut, Steviala Kristal, and vanilla aroma. Microwave the bowl (700 Watt) for a minute and set aside. If you do not have a microwave, you can also heat it short in a saucepan. In the meantime, beat the egg in some other bowl and upload the remaining whipped cream.

2. Now warmth the coconut milk and cream cheese in a saucepan till the cream cheese has melted. Then add the whipped cream with grated coconut to the pan. Heat this in short, and sooner or later, add the crushed egg with the whipped cream. Heat this whilst stirring until the pudding begins to thicken. Turn off the heat when the combination starts evolved to boil.

3. Pour the mixture into 4 small ramekins or dessert glasses and allow it to set within the fridge for at least 2 hours. Garnish the coconut pudding with a bit of grated coconut earlier than serving. Enjoy your meal!

NUTRITIONAL VALUES

Serving Size: 1 bowl
Calories: 300

Fat: 29.5
Carbohydrates: 3.6

Fiber: 2.3
Proteins: 4.1

Low-carbohydrate chocolate mousse

Cooking time: 15 mins
Total time: 135 mins

INGREDIENTS

- 250 ml of whipped cream
- 150 gr dark chocolate, 85% cocoa
- 40 - 50 g erythritol
- 3 medium eggs
- 1 tsp vanilla aroma
- pinch of salt

PREPARATION METHOD

1. Pour the whipped cream right into a big bowl. Make certain the whipped cream and bowl are cold. Beat the whipped cream with an electric-powered mixer at a medium pace and on the quit at an excessive velocity. Beat till peaks begin to shape. Do not beat too lengthy, due to the fact then a type of butter may additionally form and that is irreversible. Put the whipped cream inside the fridge after whipping

2. Fill a saucepan with a layer of water and produce it to a boil. Then place a heat-resistant bowl on the pinnacle of the saucepan and soften the dark chocolate in a bain-marie. After melting, permit the chocolate relaxation at room temperature.

3. Now get an easy heatproof bowl and add the eggs, erythritol, and salt to the bowl. Place the bowl on top of the saucepan with the boiling water, taking care not to allow the water to touch the bowl. Beat with the mixer on the very best setting, till the egg combination feels lukewarm. Then do away with the bowl from the pan and hold whisking on the counter till the aggregate has cooled down.

4. Add the melted chocolate alongside the vanilla aroma to the egg mixture and beat it properly. Finally, gently fold the whipped cream into the chocolate mixture till nicely mixed. Spoon the low-carb chocolate mousse into 6 small dessert glasses, cover with cling movie and allow it set in the fridge for at least 2 hours. Enjoy your meal!

NUTRITIONAL VALUES

Serving Size: 1 small dessert glass
Calories: 317

Fats: 29.3
Carbohydrates: 5.2

Proteins: 6.3

Lemon panna cotta

Cooking time: 5 mins

Total time: 185 mins

INGREDIENTS

- 250 ml of whipped cream
- 125 gr Greek yogurt
- 3 gelatin sheets
- 30 gr Steviala Crystal
- juice of 1 lemon
- 1 tsp grated lemon zest

PREPARATION METHOD

1. Heat the whipped cream in a pan with the steviala. Soak the gelatine sheets in cold water for 5 minutes. Squeeze the gelatin leaves and add them to the whipped cream inside the pan
2. Stir till the gelatin leaves dissolve, but don't allow it to boil. Then upload the yogurt and lemon juice whilst stirring. Mix till clean, after which eliminate the pan from the warmth.
3. Divide the cream mixture among four big or 6 small dessert glasses. Let them set in the refrigerator for at least 4 hours. Before serving, garnish the panna cotta with grated lemon zest and a lemon wedge. Enjoy your meal!

NUTRITIONAL VALUES

Serving Size: 1 bowl

Calories: 156

Fat: 15.6

Carbohydrates: 2.2

Proteins: 1.6

Low-carbohydrate almond magnums

Cooking time: 10 mins
Total time: 180 mins

INGREDIENTS

- 200 ml whipped cream
- 50 gr peanut butter
- 85 gr dark chocolate, 85% cocoa
- 1 vanilla pod
- 25 gr Steviala Crystal
- 60 ml almond milk
- 20 g almonds, chopped into pieces

PREPARATION method

1. Take a huge bowl and beat the whipped cream with an electric mixer until stiff. When the whipped cream is almost set, upload the Steviala crystal. Then upload the peanut butter and almond milk and gently stir it into the whipped cream.
2. Then region the vanilla pod on a reducing slice or plate and cut the stick open lengthwise with a pointy knife. Then spread the stick. You can see all varieties of small black seeds inside the stick. Now take a small spoon or a stupid knife and scrape out the vanilla pith (the small black seeds) and add it to the whipped cream.
3. Stir the entirety collectively nicely and divide the whipped cream mixture over 4-6 ice cream molds; depending on your molds' size. Put a stick in the ice creams and place it within the freezer for at least 3 hours.
4. Melt the chocolate au-bain, Marie, while the ice lotions are tough. When the chocolate has melted, eliminate the ice lotions from the molds. You can try this by strolling a few cold glasses of water over the molds. Place the finely chopped almonds on a plate. Then dip the ice lotions in the chocolate and then inside the finely chopped almonds. Let it harden inside the freezer and experience!

NUTRITIONAL VALUES

Serving size: 1 magnum
Calories: 254

Fat: 23.5
Carbohydrates: 3.3

Proteins: 4.1

Mascarpone dessert with berries

Cooking time: 10 mins　　　　　　　　**Total time: 10 mins**

INGREDIENTS

- 115 gr mascarpone
- 125 ml of whipped cream
- 3 tbsp Steviala Kristal or to taste
- 250 gr strawberries
- 125 gr blueberries

PREPARATION METHOD

1. In a large bowl with an electric mixer, beat the mascarpone, whipped cream, and Steviala crystal together on the highest setting till stiff peaks form.
2. Cut the strawberries into small cubes and divide them between your six maximum lovely dessert glasses. Then divide the mascarpone over the glasses and top it off with the blueberries. Enjoy your meal!

NUTRITIONAL VALUES

Serving size: 1 glass
Calories: 169

Fats: 15.2
Carbohydrates: 5.4

Proteins: 1.8

Meringue

Cooking time: 20 mins
Total time: 40 mins

INGREDIENTS

- proteins from 4 medium eggs
- Steviala crystal to taste
- few drops of lemon aroma
- 100 gr mascarpone
- 100 ml of whipped cream
- 1/2 vanilla pod or vanilla aroma
- handful of fruit

PREPARATION METHOD

1. Preheat the oven to one hundred fifty degree. Then take a massive bowl and beat the egg whites, lemon flavor, and sweetener until stiff until peaks shape. Using a serving spoon, the crushed egg whites in hundreds on a baking tin included baking paper. Then push dimples inside the mounds and bake the pastries for forty mins inside the preheated oven.
2. Then cut the vanilla pod in half lengthwise. Use the stick's give-up as a deal with, and from there, pull a knife straight via the fruit. Use the blunt aspect of your knife to take the seeds out of the stick in one cross, urgent firmly, however no longer too difficult.
3. Take a bowl and mix the mascarpone, sweetener, and vanilla nicely collectively and set it apart. Now take another big bowl and beat the whipped cream in it. Fold the whipped cream into the mascarpone. Then take the meringues out of the oven after forty minutes and allow them to cool down. After cooling, divide the sauce over the meringues and serve with a few fruits.

NUTRITIONAL VALUES

Serving Size: 1/7
Calories: 110

Fats: 10.8
Carbohydrates: 1.2

Proteins: 3.1

Vanilla coconut ice cream

Cooking time:
240 mins
Total time: 240 mins

INGREDIENTS

- 2 cans of full-fat coconut milk
- 1 tsp vanilla aroma
- erythritol or stevia to taste

PREPARATION METHOD

1. Let the cans of coconut milk stiffen in the fridge for four hours. After 4 hours, remove the cans from the fridge. Remove the lid and let the remaining liquid in the cans drain.
2. Then put the remaining coconut fat collectively with the sweetener and vanilla aroma in a blender and blend till smooth. Put the combination in a plastic container and area the box within the freezer.
3. After 45 mins, cast off the box from the freezer, stirring the combination nicely once more. The stirring ensures that it remains a thick and creamy mixture. Repeat this until the container has been within the freezer for 4 hours.

NUTRITIONAL VALUES

Serving Size: 1/5   Fats: 24.2   Proteins: 3.2
Calories: 252   Carbohydrates: 2.5

Avocado chocolate cookies

Cooking time: 10 mins   **Total time: 20 mins**

INGREDIENTS

- 3 ripe avocados
- 30 gr protein powder (chocolate flavor)
- 140 gr almond flour
- 45 gr finely ground linseed
- 5 tbsp unsweetened cocoa powder
- 70 g sugar-free chocolate, chopped into pieces
- 1 medium egg
- 1 tsp baking powder
- 3 tbsp Steviala crystal

PREPARATION METHOD

1. Preheat the oven to 180 ranges. In a bowl, mix the almond flour, linseed flour, cocoa powder, stevia, egg white powder, and baking powder collectively. Then puree the avocado and stir it into the flour combination. Finally, upload an egg and blend properly.
2. Then stir the chocolate chips into the flour and avocado mixture. Shape the dough into 18 balls on the scale of your thumb. Then flatten the balls with a rolling pin.
3. Place the flat dough balls on a baking dish lined with baking paper. Bake the cookies in the oven for 10-12 mins. Then let them calm down for a while. Enjoy your meal!

NUTRITIONAL VALUES

Serving Size: 1 biscuit   Fat: 10.0   Proteins: 4.7

Calories: 143   Carbohydrates: 5.4

Strawberries dipped in chocolate

Cooking time: 5 mins   **Total time: 10 mins**

INGREDIENTS

- 100 gr dark chocolate (85%) or sugar-free chocolate
- 12 large strawberries
- optional: coconut grater or nuts

PREPARATION METHOD

1. Cover a baking tray with parchment paper. Cut the chocolate into small portions and region in a microwave secure bowl.
2. Place the chocolate in the microwave for 1 minute. Then put off the field from the microwave and stir the whole lot together properly. Then area the bowl inside the microwave for every other 20 seconds. Stir once more after 20 seconds and on the other hand in the microwave for 20 seconds. Repeat this manner till the chocolate has melted nicely. You can also melt the chocolate in a pan in a bain-marie (over boiling water).
3. When the chocolate has melted, put off the bowl from the microwave. Now dip thirds of each strawberry in the melted chocolate and optionally in the coconut grater or chopped nuts. Drain the strawberries over the bowl and then area them on the baking tray.
4. Then positioned the baking tray inside the refrigerator and permit the strawberries to cool for a half-hour.

NUTRITIONAL VALUES

Serving Size: 4 strawberries

Fats: 3.0

Proteins: 0.5

Calories: 54

Carbohydrates: 5.2

Low-carbohydrate banana muffins

Cooking time: 15 mins   **Total time: 20 mins**

INGREDIENTS

- 200 gr almond flour
- 1 tsp baking powder
- pinch of salt

- 2 - 3 tbsp Steviala crystal
- 150 - 200 ml coconut milk

- butter for greasing
- 2 medium eggs
- 2 small ripe bananas

PREPARATION METHOD

1. Preheat the oven to a hundred and eighty degree. Then take a muffin tin for 12 portions and grease it with butter. Grab a blender and grind 1.5 bananas in it.
2. In a large bowl, combine the almond flour, baking powder, and salt. Then take some other bowl and beat together the eggs, coconut milk, finely ground banana, and Steviala crystal.
3. Carefully upload the egg aggregate to the flour and mix it. Divide the batter over the 12 ramekins and slice the last half banana. Garnish each muffin with a slice of banana. Bake the banana cakes for 20-25 mins in the preheated oven and experience!

NUTRITIONAL VALUES

Serving Size: 1 muffin   Fats: 12.0   Proteins: 4.7

Calories: 146   Carbohydrates: 6.4

Low-carbohydrate apple and cranberry cake

Cooking time: 45 mins   **Total time: 55 mins**

INGREDIENTS

- 3 - 4 medium eggs
- 350 gr applesauce, without added sugar
- 135 gr almond flour
- 2 tbsp coconut flour
- 45 gr vanilla protein powder
- 1 1/2 tsp baking powder
- 25 gr dried cranberries

PREPARATION METHOD

1. Preheat the oven to 175 degree. Then seize a bowl and blend within the eggs, baking powder, apple sauce, almond flour, protein powder, and coconut flour. Stir the contents with a whisk to a clean batter.
2. After stirring properly, upload the cranberries and stir them via the batter and set it apart. Now take a cake tin and grease it nicely with butter or oil. Pour the batter into the cake tin and unfold well. Bake the cake in the preheated oven till golden brown for about forty-five mins. After baking, allow it to cool down and cut into 14 slices.

NUTRITIONAL VALUES

Serving Size: 1 slice   Fat: 7.3   Proteins: 7.6

Calories: 120   Carbohydrates: 5.9

Low-carbohydrate cheesecake

Cooking time: 160 mins
Total time: 180 mins

INGREDIENTS

- Bottom:
- 175 gr almond flour
- pinch of salt
- 1 large egg
- 40 gr butter, melted
- 20 gr Steviala Crystal
- Cottage cheese filling:
- 500 gr low-fat cottage cheese
- 350 gr strawberries
- 250 ml of whipped cream
- 12 sheets of gelatin
- 100 ml of fresh orange juice
- 2 scoops of protein powder (vanilla or strawberry)
- dash of vanilla aroma

PREPARATION METHOD

1. Preheat the oven to a hundred and eighty degree. Take a massive bowl and blend the almond flour and salt with a whisk. Then add the big egg, Steviala Kristal, and the melted butter to the bowl and blend well. Take the cake tin and cover the lowest with baking paper. Press the dough onto the bottom of the pie crust and spread the dough frivolously. Bake the pie crust for 8 to 12 minutes inside the preheated oven.
2. Then take a bowl and fill it with cold water. Place the 12 gelatin sheets and let them soak for 5 minutes. Meanwhile, puree the 250 grams of strawberries in a blender. Put the one hundred ml sparkling orange juice in a saucepan and warm it over low heat. After 5 minutes soak, squeeze the gelatin leaves nicely. Remove the orange juice from the heat and mix inside the gelatin leaves even as stirring. Let the mixture cool.
3. In a massive bowl, stir together the low-fat quark, egg white powder, orange combination, and strawberry puree. In every other bowl, beat the whipped cream and vanilla aroma until stiff and scoop it lightly through the quark combination. Taste the aggregate and season with Steviala Kristal if vital. Divide the quark mixture over the almond base and permit it to set within the refrigerator for 3 hours.
4. After 3 hours, do away with the cheesecake from the refrigerator, reduce the final strawberries in half, and divide them over the low-carb cheesecake. Enjoy your meal!

NUTRITIONAL VALUES

Serving size: 1 slice	Fats: 26.0	Proteins: 17.3
Calories: 330	Carbohydrates: 9.5	

Vanilla blueberry muffins

Cooking time: 20 mins **Total time: 35 mins**

INGREDIENTS

- 5 medium eggs
- 1 tsp vanilla aroma
- 3 tbsp Steviala crystal
- 200 gr cream cheese
- 200 gr almond flour
- 1 tsp baking powder
- 30 gr butter
- 40 gr sugar-free chocolate
- 100 gr blueberries
- 1/2 tsp cinnamon
- pinch of salt

PREPARATION METHOD

1. Preheat the oven to 180 degree. Then mix the 5 eggs, 3 tbsp stevia, and 1 tsp vanilla aroma properly together in a bowl. Then add the 2 hundred grams of cream cheese to the bowl and mix until easy.

2. Then upload the almond flour, baking powder, cinnamon, butter, and a pinch of salt and beat till smooth. Pour the batter right into a greased muffin tray and divide the extra darkish chocolate and blueberries over the desserts. Bake the truffles for 20 to twenty-five minutes inside the preheated oven and allow them to quiet down after baking. Enjoy your meal!

NUTRITIONAL VALUES

Serving Size: 1 muffin Fats: 14.2 Proteins: 6.7

Calories: 192 Carbohydrates: 3.4

Chocolate pecan pie

Cooking time: 30 mins
Total time: 50 mins

INGREDIENTS

Bottom:

- 260 gr almond flour, extra fine
- 2 tbsp coconut oil
- 1 medium egg
- 1/8 tsp salt
- 4 tbsp Steviala Kristal or to taste

Cake filling:

- 255 gr freshly grated zucchini or courgetti
- 130 g pecans, cut in half
- 85 g sugar-free extra dark chocolate
- 6 tbsp coconut oil, melted
- 3 medium eggs
- 1 1/2 tsp vanilla flavor
- 3 - 4 tbsp Steviala Kristal or to taste
- pinch of salt

PREPARATION METHOD

1. Preheat the oven to a hundred and eighty degree Celsius. Then grease a 23 cm cake pan with a touch of coconut oil. Make the bottom by mixing the almond flour, 2 tablespoons coconut oil, a pinch of salt, and 1 egg in a bowl. When properly blended, put the dough in the cake tin and lightly press the dough towards the lowest and area.

2. Now take the grated zucchini and squeeze the moisture out of the zucchini; you could do this via carefully squeezing the zucchini in a clean kitchen towel. Then put the grated zucchini, chocolate, melted coconut oil, vanilla extract, stevia, and the three eggs in a food processor and flip it on. Mix this for approximately 1 minute.

3. Then positioned the chocolate filling in a clean bowl and stirred in seventy-five% of the pecans. Then pour the chocolate pecan combination into the pie pan and sprinkle the ultimate pecans over the pie.

4. Bake the chocolate pecan pie for 30 to forty mins within the preheated oven. The cake is exceptional after cooling it in a single day within the refrigerator. Divide the cake into 12 quantities and revel in!

NUTRITIONAL VALUES

Serving size: 1 slice

Calories: 35

7Fat: 28.3

Carbohydrates: 3.2

CONCLUSION

Many people who hear the word ketosis for the first time look a little incredulous at first. What does it actually mean to follow a ketogenic diet and what are the benefits of the diet?

The keto diet is very popular with more and more people and numerous examples show that you can burn fatter if you turn the adjusting screws of your diet. Biohackers also use the ketogenic diet to increase their cognitive performance and keep the brain running at full speed.

The keto diet will help you burn excess body fat and have more energy. We'll show you what it means to eat a ketogenic diet.

Do you know the feeling when the scale suddenly shows a few kilograms more, even though you have not eaten too much? For people who are just about to lose some weight, the excess on the scales can be a real slap in the face. If you're one of those people who is desperately looking for a diet that works, you should give the ketogenic diet a try. Diet is based on healthy fats and high-quality proteins, while you cut down on carbohydrates and turn your body into a fat-burning machine.

There are many benefits to a ketogenic diet and it gets fat burning going. It also has a positive effect on mental and physical performance. However, some experts see the low vitamin intake in comparison to the high fat and protein intake over a longer period of time very critically.

Those who are aiming for weight loss can achieve good results with this diet. The keto diet, however, brings about a profound change in metabolism. This can lead to difficulties, especially in the initial phase. If you want to try the diet, you should always do so with professional or medical advice.

CPSIA information can be obtained
at www.ICGtesting.com
Printed in the USA
BVHW011334280421
605947BV00011BA/1785